God Speaks Science

"Science and Christianity have tussled through the ages all the way from Galileo and Darwin right to the present day. With *God Speaks Science*, David Johnson presents a clearly thought-out appreciation of modern molecular biology as a celebration of the creator's plan for life. His lucid explanations and comprehensive scope provide a wonderful perspective for newcomers to molecular biology as well as those already in the field and effectively explores the quandaries at the interface of science and Christianity."

—JONATHAN M. HARRIS, professor of protein biochemistry, Queensland University of Technology

"One of the most moving and compelling verses of Scripture is 'the heavens continuously proclaim the glory of God, and the firmament perpetually recounts the work of his hands' (Ps 19:1). This marvelous volume from a distinguished hard-scientist, devout person of faith, and a cherished friend brings together the marvels of science and the truth of Scripture. The result is a wonderful volume that contributes much to the discussion of faith and science. I highly recommend it."

—CHRISTOPHER ROLLSTON, chair of classical and Near Eastern languages and civilizations, George Washington University

"In *God Speaks Science*, David Johnson provides the reader with a clear and encouraging discussion of how science is also God's expression—one of the ways he speaks and demonstrates to us the grandeur and diversity of his creation. Illustrations, examples, and video links throughout the book offer further depth and detail that connect us to God through the language of science."

—MICHAEL BRASWELL, author of *The Memory of Grace*

"I have witnessed and wept over the supposed battle of science and faith and the destruction it reaps upon the souls of mankind. David Johnson has written a wonderful and much-needed book showing that the two not only coexist but that one points to the truths of the other. This book is needed for today and can serve as a

valued window into the complementary role that science and faith play in aiding a person to find true meaning in life."
—David Clark, retired minister,
   Boones Creek Christian Church

God Speaks Science

The Simple Chemistry of Life and Faith

DAVID A. JOHNSON

Foreword by THEODORE THOMAS

RESOURCE *Publications* • Eugene, Oregon

GOD SPEAKS SCIENCE
The Simple Chemistry of Life and Faith

Copyright © 2024 David A. Johnson. All rights reserved. Except for brief quotations in critical publications or reviews, no part of this book may be reproduced in any manner without prior written permission from the publisher. Write: Permissions, Wipf and Stock Publishers, 199 W. 8th Ave., Suite 3, Eugene, OR 97401.

Resource Publications
An Imprint of Wipf and Stock Publishers
199 W. 8th Ave., Suite 3
Eugene, OR 97401

www.wipfandstock.com

PAPERBACK ISBN: 979-8-3852-1850-9
HARDCOVER ISBN: 979-8-3852-1851-6
EBOOK ISBN: 979-8-3852-1852-3

The Holy Bible, New International Version®, and NIV® are trademarks registered in the United States Patent and Trademark Office by Biblica, Inc.®: Copyright © 1973, 1978, 1984, 2011 by Biblica, Inc.™ Used by permission of Zondervan. All rights reserved worldwide. www.zondervan.com

All rights reserved.

No portion of this book may be reproduced in any form without written permission from the publisher or author, except as permitted by U.S. copyright law.

Cover image: *The Sistine Chapel ceiling in the Vatican City, Rome* by the Italian Renaissance artist Michelangelo (1475-1564 A.D.) Made 1508-12 A.D. Original image by Alonso de Mendoza, was uploaded by Mark Cartwright, and published on 17 August 2020. The copyright holder has published this content under the following license: Public Domain.

Dedicated
to
Judy, my love, and best friend
And
People of faith everywhere who love knowledge and seek truth

God's majesty is seen in the heavens, the Earth, and the atoms that make up every molecule of our physical being. Amino acids, the words of life are arranged in different sequences like words in sentences, providing form and function to every living thing.

Table of Contents

List of Illustrations and Table x
Foreword xiii
Preface xv
Acknowledgments xvii
Abbreviations xix

Chapter 1: The Mysteries and Beauty of Life 1
    Introduction 1
    Science 9
    Faith 11
    The Role of Scientists 12

Chapter 2: Science is Useful Knowledge 14
    Metabolism 14
    Proteins 15
    Sugars 16
    Fats 18
    The Importance of Diet 19
    Water, Oxygen, and Vitamins 19
    Holy Communion or the Eucharist 20

Chapter 3: Water and Hydrogen Bonds 22
    God Makes the Weak and Insignificant Important 22

Chapter 4: The Facts of Life 25
    The Genetic Alphabet and Words of Life 25
    DNA 26
    DNA Replication 28
    Translation of DNA into the Protein Sentences of Life 29

Table of Contents

    Genetic Code   31
    Mitochondrial DNA   32

Chapter 5: Proteins - the Sentences of Life   34
    Proteins Overview   34
    All Life is Made of Proteins   35
    Protein Structures   39

Chapter 6: Three Important Proteins   41
    Hemoglobin, Trypsin, and Collagen   41

Chapter 7: Hemoglobin   44
    Hemoglobin Structure   44
    Heme, Lead Poisoning, Purple Urine, and Vampires   46
    Sickle Cell Anemia   48
    Blue People of Kentucky   49
    Hemoglobin and Jaundice   51
    Hemoglobin A1c and Diabetes   51

Chapter 8: Enzymes   53
    Trypsin Example of an Enzyme   53
    The Most Important Enzyme on Earth   56

Chapter 9: Collagen   58
    Collagen the Structural Protein   58
    Osteogenesis Imperfecta-Fragile Bones   60
    Cartilage Cushions Joints   60
    Scurvy   61

Chapter 10: Blood- the Stream of Life   63
    Blood Cells   63
    Blood Cell Diversity   64

Chapter 11: Red Blood Cells   66
    Red Blood Cells   66
    Carbon Dioxide Transport   67
    Heme Disposal and O_2 Saturation Measurement   68

Chapter 12: Infection Fighters   70
    Neutrophils Fight Infection   70
    Plasma Cells and Vaccinations   71

Table of Contents

Chapter 13: Blood Clotting 72
    Platelets Plug Cuts 72
    Rat Poison Discovery 73
    Hemophilia and the Russian Revolution 74
    Endothelium the Blood Vessel Lining 75
    Nitroglycerin and Angina 75

Chapter 14: Hydrogen Bonds in DNA 77
    PCR Revolutionized the Study of DNA 77

Chapter 15: Proteins: Chains of Amino Acids 80
    Linking Amino Acids Together 80
    Alpha Helix 82
    Beta Sheet 83
    Amino Acid Structures – The Words of Life 84
    Disulfide Bonds 85

Chapter 16: Proteins and Diet 86
    Nine Amino Acids Are Essential for Humans 86
    Milk 87
    Eggs 89

Chapter 17: Creation and Science 91
    Creation of Humans with Souls 91
    Genesis Creation Stories 94
    Evolution is Not Scary 96
    Genetic Diversity Makes Life Beautiful 97
    The Bible is Not a Science Book 98
    Good News in the Gospels 100

Chapter 18: Interesting Scientific Facts 103
    Viruses are Not Alive 103
    Mad Cow Disease and Alzheimer's 104

Chapter 19: Science Gives Hope 106
    Science and Hope 106
    Vaccines Prevent Disease and Save Money 107
    RNA Vaccines, asRNA, and siRNA Drugs 108
    Monoclonal Antibodies 109
    Synthetic Peptide Drugs 110

Table of Contents

 CRISPR-Cas9 110
 Artificial Intelligence (AI) 111

Chapter 20: A Personal Journey with Science and Faith 114
 Education, Family, and Faith 114
 Lung Biochemistry and Emphysema Research 115
 Research at East Tennessee State University 117
 Our Church, Faith, and Community 118

Figures, images, and video preparation 119
My YouTube Channel 120
Bibliography 123

List of Illustrations and Table

01. How God Created All Life
02. God Created the Cosmos
03. Basic Metabolism
04. Water
05. DNA Structure
06. DNA transcription and mRNA translation into Protein
07. mRNA
08. Codon Table
09. Protein Polypeptide
10. Troponin Sequence Alignment
11. Amino Acid Abbreviations
12. Human Hemoglobin
13. Heme
14. Sickle Cell Hb
15. Blue People Gene Pedigree
16. Human Trypsin
17. RuBisCo
18. Collagen
19. Blood Cells
20. Blood Cells EM
21. RBC Carbonic anhydrase
22. Lung Alveolus
23. DNA Hydrogen Bonding
24. PCR
25. Amino Acid Structure
26. Alpha Helix

List of Illustrations and Table

27. Beta Sheet
28. Amino Acids
29. God is Visible in the Molecules of Life
30. Hemoglobin A1c
31. Blood Clotting Made Simple
32. Factor 5 Leiden

Table 1: Milks Approximate Content per cup (240ml)

Foreword

I SEE DAVID JOHNSON almost every Wednesday morning when we meet for breakfast at Bob Evans. After coffee, bacon, and eggs, we and ten other men huddle around a book of the Bible. We pray together. We are a diverse group. One of us is a retired appellate judge; another is in real estate; one man was in retail trade for decades; one used to clean up toxic waste sites; one is a cattle breeder, another a salesman, another an educator, another an engineer, still another knows all about computers. Frequently we'll have questions for each other that draw on our various fields of expertise. So, when it comes to questions about the natural sciences, Professor Johnson is our go-to guy. David knows that his colleagues around the breakfast table do not live in biochemistry labs, so he keeps his answers on the "popular" level, avoiding the professional language that would overwhelm us all.

To explain the wonders of biochemistry to me, David has his work cut out. Even in high school, I would have regarded "simple chemistry" as an oxymoron. As a historian and theologian, I dabble in half a dozen languages, but laboratory lingo is not among them, so David has to work cleverly to put the wonderful concepts of biochemistry into speech I can understand. Sometimes he just cannot help himself, and phrases like "heme disposal" and "trypsin is a protease enzyme" and "monoclonal antibodies" spill out of his mouth. My favorite David-ism is "osteogenesis imperfecta" and "retinitis pigmentosa." Such vocabulary amazes me! (I secretly wonder if David would be reciprocally amazed at my description of "apostas" as a fine example of an aorist active participle nominative singular iteration of "aphistemi." Or if he appreciates the controversy surrounding DSS 7Q5.)

So, for my benefit, David inventively describes trypsin as an enzyme that cuts up proteins like a saw cuts up lumber into the precisely shaped boards that go into building my house. THAT I can understand!

Behind every one of David's explanations of how biology and chemistry cooperate is a reverence for the Creator. In God Speaks Science: The Simple Chemistry of Life and Faith, Prof. Johnson anticipates the questions that honest truth-seekers might ask about this liminal territory where physics and metaphysics walk side by side. Through this book, his students, in particular, get a glimpse of the thoughtful human being, the conscientious child of God, who lives inside the white lab coat.

—By Dr. Theodore Thomas, Milligan College Emeritus Professor of Humanities, History and German

Preface

*"The heavens declare the glory of God; the skies proclaim the work of his hands. Day after day they pour forth speech; night after night they reveal knowledge." (Psalm 19:1-2)*1.

THIS BOOK IS BASED on faith in God as the creator of the earth, the universe, and the cosmos. The simplicity and the majesty of creation can be seen in the molecules of life, the proteins that make up every living thing on Earth. The enormity of the cosmos speaks to the power of God who sent His Son Jesus to replace the laws of man with just two commands, love God and love one another. Creation at the molecular level may seem mysterious, but it is no more mysterious than visions of majestic mountains, expansive plains, and deep blue seas. Faith and science are simple. God used just a four-letter alphabet (DNA) and a vocabulary of just twenty words (amino acids) to speak all life into existence. Who created the universe is based on faith because science can neither prove nor disprove who created all we know. Whether one believes in a six-day creation or some evolving process, the chemistry of life as we know it today is presented. God designed life's molecules with the ability to change just as He made humans with the power to heal and become more loving of others. The importance of weak hydrogen bonds to the structures of water, DNA, and proteins, shows how God wonderfully used weakness to make molecules, just as He has used many weak people to do great things. The 3D structures of many proteins are now known. Amino acids are

Preface

arranged in different sequences in proteins as words are mixed to write varied sentences. Clear explanations are provided concerning topics including metabolism, nutrition, blood cells, hemoglobin, collagen, and enzymes, along with health-related information, such as hemoglobin A1c, purple urine, vampire origins, blood clotting, rat poison, diabetes, viruses, mad cow disease, Alzheimer's, vaccines, antibody therapies, recent drug advances, CRISPR-Cas9 gene editing, and AI-powered protein modeling. Included are some interesting stories learned during many years of teaching medical biochemistry. Everyone can benefit from a basic understanding of the molecules and cells that keep them alive. There are several color images and videos to enhance the learning experience. QR codes link to YouTube Unlisted videos by the author that show all the figures in color and provide brief explanations of the figure or molecule. Videos were designed to show the enormity of the cosmos, and the beauty of DNA, proteins, water, and other molecules. Videos labeled Short are YouTube Shorts (less than one minute). Biblical and spiritual quotations connect science and faith for Christians of all ages and religious sects, as well as others.

Acknowledgments

MANY THANKS TO DR. Michael Braswell, a longtime friend and ETSU faculty colleague, for encouraging me to write this book and providing advice about formatting and publishing. Perry Rindfleisch, my brother in Christ, read an early draft and gave some sage advice. Comments and edits by Judy, my wonderful wife and life partner were invaluable. Granddaughter Genevieve provided a younger person's perspective. Dr. Theodore Thomas, (ordained minister, missionary in Germany, humanities professor, and friend) carefully read and edited the manuscript, and guided me to useful Biblical references. David Clark, our minister at Boones Creek Christian Church for 22 years, encouraged me in many ways. He often said, "Anywhere you cut the Bible it bleeds Jesus.". Thanks to Dr. Thomas Ecay, a colleague and physiologist at Quillen College of Medicine for advice concerning protein nutrition. Professor Johnathan Harris has been a wonderful scientific collaborator and friend via email. His perspectives from the other side of the world have been a blessing. Dr. Christopher Rollston is a brilliant scholar of Near Eastern Languages, a church friend, and an ordained minister, who had a positive influence on my faith Thanks to Dr. J. Kelly Smith, M.D. who diagnosed my heart issue in his office down the hall and drove me to the hospital, saving me from a stroke or heart attack. Thanks also to my daughter Susannah who noticed that I was breathing hard after climbing stairs and for insisting I see Dr. Smith, a mentor to her in medical school. Growing up in a Christian home in the U.S.A. was like winning the lottery. Our three children, Colin, Nicholas, and Susannah, along

Acknowledgments

with their spouses have enriched our lives. One purpose of this book is to pass on some knowledge and faith to our grandchildren, from Pops with much love. The author's royalties will be donated to church or local charities.

Abbreviations

Adenosine triphosphate (ATP)
Alanine (Ala or A)
Alpha-1 Antitrypsin (A1AT)
Amyloid precursor protein (APP)
Amyloid beta (Aβ)
Antisense RNA (asRNA)
Arginine (Arg or R)
Artificial Intelligence (AI)
Asparagine (Asn or N)
Aspartic Acid (Asp or D)
Boones Creek Christian Church (BCCC)
Bovine Spongiform Encephalopathy (BSE)
Centers for Disease Control and Prevention (CDC)
Cysteine (Cys or C)
Deoxyribonucleic acid (DNA)
Digestible Indispensable Amino Acid Score (DIAAS)
Glucose-dependent insulinotropic polypeptide (GIP)
Glucagon-like peptide-1 (GLP-1)
Glutamic Acid (Glu or E)
Glutamine (Gln or Q)
Glycine (Gly or G)
Hemoglobin A1c (A1c)
High fructose corn syrups (HFCS)
Histidine (His or H)
Hydrogen bonds (H-bonds)
Isoleucine (Ile or I)

Abbreviations

Leucine (Leu or L)
Low-density lipoprotein (LDL)
Lysine (Lys or K)
Measles, mumps, and rubella vaccine (MMR)
Messenger ribonucleic acid (mRNA
Methionine (Met or M))
Nitric oxide (NO)
Phenylalanine (Phe or F)
Proline (Pro or P)
Protein Data Bank (PDB)
Red blood cells (RBCs)
Ribonucleic acid (RNA)
Ribulose-1,5-bisphosphate carboxylase/oxygenase (RuBisCo)
Serine (Ser or S)
SERine Proteinase INhibitors (SERPINs)
Polymerase Chain Reaction (PCR)
small interfering RNA (siRNA)
Threonine (Thr or T)
Transfer RNAs (tRNAs)
Tryptophan (Trp or W)
Tyrosine (Tyr or Y)
Valine (Val or V)
variant Creutzfeldt-Jakob Disease (vCJD)
Wisconsin Alumni Research Foundation (WARF and WARFarin)
White blood cells (WBCs)

CHAPTER 1

The Mysteries and Beauty of Life

"What kind of artistry is equal to the silver glisten on a river, or a sunset, or lightning in the sky? What kind of man's artistry can compare to the great artistry of Creation?"
—BOB DYLAN- SINGER, SONGWRITER, NOBEL LAUREATE.[1]

Introduction

SCIENCE HAS LONG BEEN seen as a barrier or threat to religion, but our view of the world is all about wonder in both realms. In this treatise, I aim to try and clarify why faith and testable scientific hypotheses are interrelated. Our human bodies are God-created complex machines comprised of millions of components. This book is about understanding the biochemical reactions occurring within us from the point of view of a research scientist. It is an attempt to show how the remarkably simple building blocks of life are intertwined and used to sustain life. The book explains how we all have the same fundamental parts and explains how these can change over time. Scientific exploration is the unraveling of biological mysteries. Just as detectives investigate to solve crimes, scientists spend their time studying how things work. Biochemists,

---

1. Dylan, "On this day, webpage 1990."

like me, work to understand the physical aspects of the body at the molecular level.

The genesis of this book was a church communion meditation presented in April of 2016 that developed into a YouTube video titled "God is Visible in the Molecules of Life - DNA and Proteins". There is a link to this video at the end of the book, but the basic ideas are in How God Created All Life a Short YouTube Video with a QR code.

How God Created All Life

God's 4 Letter DNA Alphabet
A - Adenine
T - Thymine
G - Guanine
C - Cytosine

God's 20 Words of Life – Amino Acids
Gly-Ala-Val-Leu-Ile-Ser-Thr-Cys-Met-Pro
Asp-Asn-Glu-Gln-Phe-Tyr-Trp-His-Lys-Arg

Hemoglobin Molecule

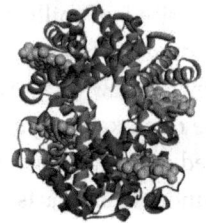

After becoming a Christian at age 11, earning BS and Ph.D. degrees in chemistry, I taught the biochemistry of proteins and amino acid metabolism at a medical school for 44 years. As a

The Mysteries and Beauty of Life

Christian, I believe Jesus is the Son of God, and as the Bible states Jesus participated in the creation process. *"In the beginning was the Word, and the Word was with God, and the Word was God. He was with God in the beginning. Through him all things were made; without him, nothing was made that has been made. In him was life, and that life was the light of all mankind. The light shines in the darkness, and the darkness has not overcome it."* (John 1:1–5, NIV). Jesus Christ is the Word and the Light. As a scientist, I see the beauty of creation in the protein molecules that make up our bodies and keep us alive. To me, the four bases of DNA comprise the alphabet of life, whereas the twenty amino acids of proteins are the words of life, just as different sentences are different arrangements of words. The varied order in which amino acids are arranged in different proteins results in each protein having a unique beautiful 3D structure. It is hoped that this book will in some small measure bridge the gap between religion and science. Just as God sees each of us as a divine soul, we need to recognize that we all contain the same intricate protein molecules that give us life.

We all marvel at the beauty of creation in our world, the moon, and stars. How and when the Earth was created is a mystery that mankind has sought to answer. Whether you believe in a six-day creation as presented in the book of Genesis, in some form of evolution, or some other process, this book will truthfully present the molecules critical to all life on Earth. The Bible, many other religious texts, and various cultures credit a higher power as the creator. As a Christian, I believe that God created the Earth, and the infinite cosmos, but as a scientist that is impossible to prove, and no experiments prove or disprove the existence of God. The Bible is all about God, and man's spiritual relationship to God, rather than about Earth's physical creation. As the Bible states Jesus Christ participated in the creation process. *"The Son is the image of the invisible God, the firstborn over all creation. For in him, all things were created: things in heaven and on earth, visible and invisible, whether thrones or powers or rulers or authorities; all things have been created through him and for him."* (Colossians 1:15–16, NV). Astronomers theorize but cannot prove that the cosmos began about thirteen billion years ago, but they lack evidence concerning who created it or how it was created. What you believe about creation and the creator is not in conflict with science, which is about the testable and physical realm of life not about the spiritual realm. No matter what you believe about the spiritual realm of life, the molecules that make life possible are no longer unknown or unseen. It is possible to see the beauty and simplicity of the structure and function of the molecules that make up all life. As a scientist, I do not think that the molecules of life just happened into existence, but that they were thoughtfully created with the capacity to evolve and improve. God has always wanted man to be spiritually better, so why wouldn't He also create us so we can also become physically better?

The God who created our planet and the Milky Way with approximately 100 billion stars of which our Sun is just one, is difficult for us to grasp. The new James Webb telescope has already discovered six massive galaxies beyond the Milky Way that are estimated to be over 500 million years old.[2] The closest star beyond our solar system is Proxima Centauri which is 4.24 light-years away. Our Milky Way is 100,000 light-years across, and light from a star on the far side that is seen today left there about 95,000 years ago during the last ice age when mammoths were still roaming the Earth. It is estimated that the Milky Way contains some 100 to 400 billion stars with as many as 40 billion like our Sun with planets.[3] So, the enormity of outer space taxes our minds to even comprehend it. God created far more than what was known when the Bible was written.

Mankind has long struggled to understand creation and the mind of God who created our Earth and all life forms. Christians, Jews, and Muslims all worship one God. The Biblical patriarch Abraham is credited with being the first to realize that there is only one God. Given the vastness of our universe, the Milky Way, and galaxies beyond, it seems almost impossible to understand the mind of God the creator of it all. God's mind is enormous

---

2. Labbé, "Population of Red," 266–69.

3. Bovy, and Rix, "A Direct Dynamical Measurement."

compared to ours, but our pride leads us to think we might understand His thoughts. *"For my thoughts are not your thoughts, neither are your ways my ways," declares the Lord. "As the heavens are higher than the earth, so are my ways higher than your ways and my thoughts than your thoughts."* (Isaiah 55:8-9, NIV). Our humanity limits our focus and ability to fully understand the awesome power of God, the creator of billions of stars in a cosmos that extends billions of light-years in every direction. God has done and can do far more than we imagine. *"The heavens declare the glory of God; the skies proclaim the work of his hands."* (Psalm 19:1, NIV). *"When I consider your heavens, the work of your fingers, the moon and the stars, which you have set in place, what is mankind that you are mindful of them, human beings that you care for them."* (Psalm 8:3-4, NIV). Christians know that God is Love and that Jesus Christ was the embodiment of that love, as Saint Augustine said, *"God Loves each of us as if there was only one of us."*[4]. This video using images from the Hubble and Webb telescopes will help convey the huge expanse of the cosmos.

God Created the Cosmos and Billions of Stars

Our Sun is One Star in The Milky Way

The Bible tells us that God is Love and that we were created in the image of God, who endowed us with the capacity to love others and to care for them at our own expense. Jesus, His Son,

4. Augustine, "God Loves Each."

came as an infant and his teachings of how to love one another have changed the world for the better. Millions of Christians have sacrificially cared for others following the example of Jesus' sacrifice for God's children. Mankind is still imperfect and even devout Christians struggle to love others as Jesus taught. Living things are amazingly complex and beautiful too; lofty, and diverse trees, myriads of colorful flowers, scores of wild animals, and dazzling ocean life. Even more mind-boggling than outer space are the trillions upon trillions of beautiful molecules that make up our bodies, and work together so we can move, breathe, and think. Love for our family, friends, and our pets provides rich rewards in life. Life is fascinating and humans have long desired to know more about the origins of the universe, as well as our existence and genesis. Science is beginning to provide insights in this regard, but science is limited to testable hypotheses. God speaks every language on earth, and the Bible teaches us about our relationship to God. He also reveals himself to us through literature, art forms, music, and science. God is the supreme physicist, mathematician, chemist, and molecular biologist. Compared to God's capacity for creation, ours is microscopic. As a chemist, biochemist, and molecular biologist, I have spent my life studying how the human body works via the myriad chemical reactions of life, and I still do not fully understand the chemistry of life.

A beautiful simplicity pervades the molecules that unite living organisms in their design. This book will explain what we currently understand about how the molecules of DNA and the amino acids of proteins unite all life. Science cannot tell us who created life or why we exist, but it does speak to the brilliance of the Creator. God made the solar system with planets revolving around the Sun, the energy source of the plants that we depend on for sustenance. Just as God is visible in the universe, He is also visible in the minute chemistry of molecules. When God spoke life into existence, He used the four molecules of DNA and twenty amino acids words. Water, which makes up about 60% of our body is the most essential molecule for life. This simple molecule has only three atoms, one oxygen, and two hydrogens. All known life forms require water. God designed water, endowing it with unique chemical properties critical to its function.

Although biochemistry and molecular biology may seem extremely complicated, the same four molecules of DNA and the same twenty amino acids are the essence of all living creatures. Do not concern yourself with memorizing any chemical names that are presented. You can understand the biology of life without understanding chemistry. A major purpose of this book is to make creation at the molecular level understandable by non-scientists and to truthfully present the facts of science. This book should be of use to young people beginning to study the biology of life, and to everyone interested in their health and nutrition. Health is important to us all, and the knowledge you will gain will help you advocate for your health and that of your loved ones. It provides a starting point to help you understand more complex health-related information. The chemical reactions that keep us alive are catalyzed by thousands of enzyme proteins, and biochemists spend their lives studying each reaction in detail. However, note that all life uses water, DNA, and just twenty amino acids. There is often an interesting story behind scientific discoveries because scientists, like all humans, are complex creatures with their own life stories. Some medical advances come about through the study of genetic abnormalities called "experiments of nature" and some have significant impacts on families and even world history. Alpha-1 Antitrypsin (A1AT) is a blood protein, and a genetic deficiency of A1AT was found to contribute to the early development of emphysema. Studies of the A1AT protein resulted in an understanding of the mechanism by which it inhibits neutrophil elastase to prevent emphysema. Also, my research on the structure and function of A1AT discovered how smoking causes emphysema.[5]

You can understand a lot about life by knowing the unique structure of water, the 4 letters of DNA, examples of three proteins (hemoglobin, enzymes, collagen), and a few blood cells. These simple topics will allow you to understand how God used weak and simple forces to make life possible. You will learn some of the

---

5. Johnson and Travis, "Structural evidence for methionine," 7142–4.

basics of nutrition and metabolism, so you can understand the importance of diet. You will also learn the basics of diabetes, hemoglobin A1C, blood clotting, blood cells, how DNA is amplified from fingerprints to solve crimes, how hemoglobin carries oxygen, the structure of your bones, and a few interesting diseases. Drug companies now advertise on TV and actors often say, "I lowered my A1c." So why is A1c so important? Short videos will explain some of the topics, just as Jesus used short stories to teach important ideas.

Jesus said, *"Then you will know the truth, and the truth will set you free."* (John 8:32, NIV). Some Christians accept the six-day creation stories in the Bible, and other Christians believe that God used evolution to create the diverse life forms seen on Earth. Neither evolution nor faith in the creation story changes the scientific information to be presented about the molecules of life. This book includes several interesting stories discovered during my 44 years of teaching medical students along with practical scientific information.

As a protein scientist, to me, the beauty of life is in the protein structures and their amazing functions. Hemoglobin in our red blood cells transports oxygen around our bodies and our metabolic enzymes turn the foods we eat into bone and muscle. Proteins are responsible for our outward appearance, skin, hair, and eyes. Proteins are made of strings of amino acids in precise order like the words in sentences. Whereas we struggle to communicate using a 26-letter alphabet and our dictionaries have thousands of words, the language of life uses just a four-letter alphabet and a twenty-word vocabulary. *"In the beginning, God created the heavens and the earth. Now the earth was formless and empty, darkness was over the surface of the deep, and the Spirit of God was hovering over the waters. And God said, "Let there be light," and there was light. God saw that the light was good, and he separated the light from the darkness. God called the light "day," and the darkness he called "night." And there was evening, and there was morning—the first day."* (Genesis 1:1–5, NIV) God created the world by just speaking. Words are powerful and just as God used words to create the world, Jesus' words changed the world for the better.

Only three letters of DNA are used to tell the protein synthesis machinery of all living cells the order in which amino acids are to be strung together (like pearls on a string) to make proteins. Christianity has three integral aspects; God, Jesus Christ, and the Holy Spirit, that work together like the three bases that code for each amino acid word. Faith, hope, and love, like the molecules that make up our bodies, bond us to God and to our fellow man, enriching our lives and making us more than a mixture of chemicals.

Science

Science is based on observations, experimentation, and the careful gathering of evidence to formulate hypotheses and testable theories. Objective logical reasoning and repeatability of experiments are critical in testing hypotheses. Scientific claims can be tested by other scientists and if new evidence contradicts a scientific theory, it may be revised or discarded. When the preponderance of data supports a hypothesis, it becomes a scientific law. For example: Newton's law of universal gravitation describes gravity as an attractive force existing between two bodies with mass. Observations of the moon's orbit, the tides, and the orbits of the planets in our solar system supported the validity of Newton's law, as well as Henry Cavendish's 1798 experiment measuring the slight gravitational force between two small lead balls. Evidence for scientific claims undergoes rigorous scrutiny by the scientific community in a process known as peer review. Before publication scientific papers are reviewed by other scientists with expertise in the area being investigated, and authors are often asked to address questions of data completeness, accuracy, and interpretation. Major scientific advances depend on the experiments of others. Scientific conclusions are frequently challenged by other scientists, and then added to and corrected in subsequent publications by other scientists. No one has ever designed a perfect experiment, and I encouraged my students to devise and perform experiments as fast as possible because we learn more from our mistakes and failures than from our successes. An undocumented quote that is often attributed to the great inventor Thomas A. Edison says " *I didn't fail 1,000 times, I didn't fail once, I succeeded in proving 1,000 ways how something couldn't be done.*" And "*I didn't fail 1000 times. The light bulb was an invention with 1000 steps.*"[6] Sometimes scientists may be totally or partially wrong in their conclusions and papers will be retracted or corrected.

Even when errors are corrected in scientific literature, they sometimes persist in the public domain. A classic example is the 1998 claim by Dr. Andrew Wakefield published in *The Lancet*,[7] suggesting that the measles, mumps, and rubella vaccine (MMR) given to children at 12–18 months of age was causing autism. Wakefield's study was flawed because it was based on only 12 children, and it wrongly concluded that the MMR vaccine was causing autism just because the first signs of autism were being recognized in children around the time of their MMR vaccination. It was erroneous to assume that vaccinations caused autism just because it was manifesting after vaccination. One might catch a cold a couple of days after a cool rainy day, but the cold virus is not in the rain; we catch cold viruses from others. Likewise, just because autism occurs sometime after vaccinations does not mean that the vaccination causes autism. The Lancet retracted the article in 2010[8], following a thorough investigation of the facts. Yet, this myth lives on, and this myth has led to unvaccinated children dying needlessly of measles. Before 1963 measles was common in the United States, sickening 3–4 million people annually, resulting in 400–500 deaths. About 1,000 people (usually children) were annually disabled due to brain damage. Measles is about six times more contagious than COVID-19, and 9 out of 10 susceptible persons with close contact develop measles. Vaccines cannot give one the disease they are designed to prevent because vaccines are made

6. Edison, "I didn't fail 1000".
7. Wakefield et al., "Ileal-lymphoid-nodular," 637–41.
8. Lancet, "Retraction, Ileal-lymphoid-nodular," 445.

of dead or crippled viruses, and extensive vaccine testing is done to be sure that vaccines cannot cause infection. Vaccines are not infectious because they are either damaged viruses or small parts of viruses, and they are thoroughly tested for infectivity before approval. Viruses must infect certain cells to replicate because they lack the metabolic and protein synthesis machinery found in our cells. Viruses use our cellular machinery and our energy to make thousands of new viral particles which escape infecting more cells. They usually damage or kill the cells they infect and that makes us ill. A 95% vaccination rate is needed to prevent measles, and the US had zero cases in 2000 due to vaccinations. In recent years cases have increased mostly due to non-vaccination, and there have been outbreaks in several foreign countries. The annual number of US cases has ranged from a low of 37 in 2004 to a high of 1,282 in 2019[9].

Faith

Faith is a spiritual plane of thinking that relies on religious texts, belief in the unknown and the untestable, and faith is based on personal beliefs, personal revelations, and traditions. Faith does not rely on empirical testing, and it tends to be resistant to change in the face of conflicting scientific evidence. Faith frequently relies on authority figures, such as religious leaders, and often uses sacred texts as sources of knowledge and guidance, but religious leaders are slow to accept scientific evidence that is contrary to their beliefs. The lives of billions of Christians over two thousand years attest to the power of Jesus Christ whose resurrection gives us hope and who sent the Holy Spirit to give us a peace that passes all understanding. *"We are not human beings having a spiritual experience. We are spiritual beings having a human experience."* Attributed to Pierre Teilhard de Chardin (French Jesuit priest,

---

9. CDC, Measles for Healthcare.

scientist, paleontologist, theologian, philosopher, and teacher; 1881–1955)[10].

At one time the Catholic church held that the Sun revolved around the Earth, based on its appearance each day in the east and setting in the west. Galileo's view that the Sun, rather than the Earth was the center of our solar system and the Earth revolved around the Sun resulted in conflict with the Catholic Church's assumptions and he was tried by the Inquisition in 1633 which forced him to recant his views. It took centuries for the Church to change its stance, but in 1992 Pope Paul II expressed regret concerning how Galileo was treated and admitted the Church had been in error. We now know that Galileo was correct.

Science and religion should not conflict because each plays a different role in life. Just as science is limited to explaining the natural world, faith's role is to give our lives a depth and richness that transcends testable knowledge. Christians hold different beliefs about the age of the earth, but we all see God's hand in the beauty of creation. Some churches have the following mantra that has been attributed to various Christian theologians, *"In essentials unity, in non-essentials liberty, and in all things love."* We all agree that salvation is the grace of God poured out through the death and resurrection of Jesus Christ. BioLogos.org is an organization started by scientists who are Christians who work for harmony in science and biblical faith.

The Role of Scientists

We scientists are truly fortunate to spend our days following our curiosity. Few people on earth are so privileged, and we consequently feel a responsibility to work hard to find answers to questions that will improve the lives of others. Scientists are also committed to passing on their knowledge to the next generation of doctors and scientists who will discover new treatments for diseases while advancing and improving on what we know today. Science is based

---

10. Teilhard, "We are not human".

on logic and our conclusions are based on the most likely explanation of available data. When multiple choices concerning the solution to a scientific question are presented, the simple choice that unites the data into a logical conclusion has been proven to be the most correct answer. Occam's Razor or principle of parsimony is a well-known philosophical principle that holds that when faced with competing explanations for a phenomenon, the simplest one is most likely to be true. It is the explanation with the fewest assumptions. To work with students and seeing them realize their dreams has been an added blessing for me. As a life-long Christian, I felt a need to use my abilities to encourage others to gain the knowledge and skills to care for the sick or to perform research that could lead to medical or scientific advances. Jesus performed some 40 miracles recorded in the Gospels. In Jesus' time, leprosy was a feared condition. Lepers were ostracized and the law forbade others from touching them. *"A man with leprosy came and knelt before him and said, "Lord, if you are willing, you can make me clean." Jesus reached out his hand and touched the man. "I am willing," he said. "Be clean!" Immediately he was cleansed of his leprosy."* (Matthew 8:2–3, NIV). Jesus did not need to touch him to heal his leprosy, but by touching him Jesus demonstrated His love and acceptance for all humanity, even those shunned by society. Medical students are taught that touching patients while performing physical exams builds a bond with the patient, demonstrating care and acceptance. The Bible records many miracles of healing, and we still pray for miracles. God has given us the ability to understand the intricacies of human metabolism and diseases resulting in new medical procedures and medications that are modern-day miracles.

CHAPTER 2

Science is Useful Knowledge

"Knowledge is power. Information is liberating. Education is the premise of progress, in every society, in every family."
—KOFI ANNAN, SECRETARY-GENERAL OF THE UNITED NATIONS[1]

Metabolism

A BASIC UNDERSTANDING OF the cells and molecules that make up our bodies will provide you with information about how your body works and this knowledge will aid communication with physicians concerning your health or the health of a loved one. Consequently, you will be introduced to several interesting cells and molecules that will help you understand the makeup and function of the body. Our bodies are our houses which are maintained by the foods we eat, so understanding basic metabolic processes can benefit health and nutrition. Our bodies are composed of about 30 trillion cells, in which about a billion biochemical reactions occur every second, even as we sleep. The architectural plans for each cell are encoded in the DNA housed in the nucleus. Proteins are

---

1. Annan, "Knowledge Is Power."

the building material of our cells, organs, and bones, and like the wooden boards used to build houses the proteins we eat must be cut up into amino acids that are absorbed into our blood and then used by our cells to build new proteins. Here are some examples of our food groups.

- **Carbohydrates:** bread, pasta, rice, potatoes, fruit, vegetables
- **Proteins:** meat, fish, poultry, eggs, dairy products, legumes
- **Fats:** butter, oil, margarine, nuts, seeds, avocados.

Fats are the richest source of energy because they are not oxidized and they give us 9 calories per gram, whereas sugars and proteins yield only 4 calories per gram. *"For we know that if the earthly tent we live in is destroyed, we have a building from God, an eternal house in heaven, not built by human hands."* (2 Corinthians 5:1, NIV)

Proteins

When we eat proteins from animals or vegetables these proteins are cut up into individual amino acids by molecular saws called proteases (enzymes) in our digestive tract. Amino acids then enter our blood, and they are carried to our different cells to build the proteins prescribed by our DNA. Our bodies can make only 11 of the 20 amino acids, so our diets must contain the 9 amino acids that we cannot make. They are termed essential amino acids and a deficiency of any one of them can result in muscle wasting because muscle is the only way we have of storing amino acids. If we eat more protein than needed the excess is converted to glucose which is the major fuel used by our brains and muscles. The liver is our most important metabolic organ, and it stores excess glucose as glycogen (glucose polymers) that can be converted to free glucose when needed. Marathon runners eat lots of pasta and other carbohydrate-rich foods before a race to store up glycogen in the liver and muscle. When our diets contain more proteins, carbohydrates, or fats than we need they are converted to fats that are stored in our cells and these can be used later for energy. The main energy molecule is ATP (adenosine triphosphate). Like a fireplace in a house, we burn our fuels via oxidation to make molecules (ATP) that our muscles use for movement, our brains need for thinking, and to keep us warm. The oxygen to burn our fuels is transported by the hemoglobin in our red blood cells. Carbon dioxide (CO_2) and water (H_2O) are the waste products that we exhale via our lungs and kidneys. The nitrogen atoms from the proteins and DNA we eat are converted by the liver to urea which is secreted via the kidneys.

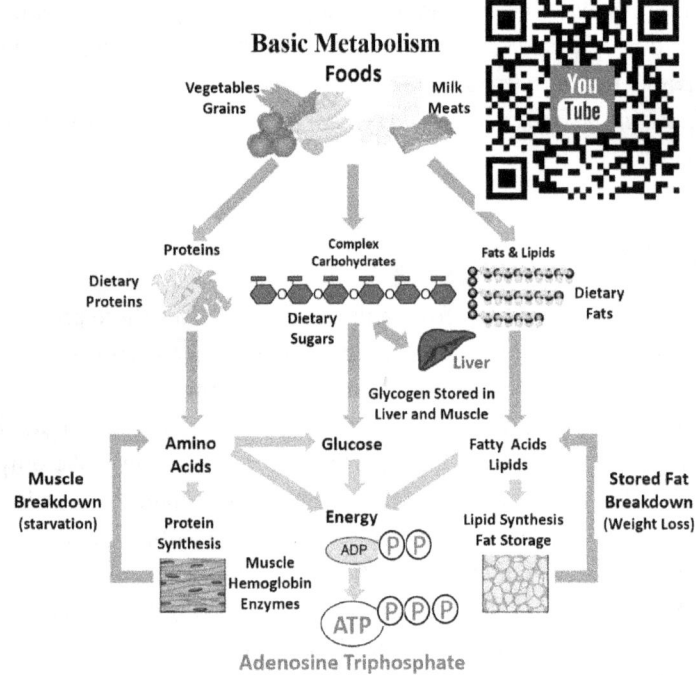

Sugars

The two main sugars in our diets are sucrose and high-fructose corn syrup. Sucrose, from sugar cane or sugar beets, is comprised of two sugars called glucose and fructose that are linked together.

Sucrose metabolism starts when sucrase, an enzyme in the intestines, splits it apart into glucose and fructose. Glucose is the primary sugar energy source of the body, especially the brain, and it requires insulin to enter our cells. Until the 19th century, sugar was a rare commodity. Sugar plantations were first established in the Mediterranean region by the Arabs in the 7th century using slave labor. The European colonization of tropical regions in the Americas led to a large increase in sugar production using enslaved Africans to work the sugar cane plantations under cruel conditions. Sugar beet cultivation in more moderate climates accounts for about 40% of sucrose production today, but sugar cane cultivation in tropical climates results in higher yields per acre.

Fructose is primarily metabolized in the liver, and it does not need insulin to enter cells. Fructose can result in the accumulation of fat in the liver, which can lead to non-alcoholic fatty liver disease. High fructose corn syrup is used as a sweetener in many products, such as candy and beverages because fructose tastes sweeter than sucrose. Tariffs that raised the price of imported cane sugar and farm subsidies for raising corn have resulted in corn being used to make high fructose corn syrups (HFCS), as substitutes for sucrose. Corn starch is a polymer of glucose and the enzyme alpha-amylase is used to break down the starch into individual glucose molecules. Pure glucose is seldom used as a sweetener because gram for gram it is only about 75% as sweet as sucrose. Fructose tastes about 1.5 times sweeter than sucrose. The enzyme invertase is then used to convert some of the glucose to fructose. Alpha-amylase and invertase are usually purified from bacteria and yeasts, but recombinant enzymes can also be used. Economics and science have combined to convert glucose from corn starch to fructose. High fructose corn syrups (HFCS) with up to 90% fructose can be made in these industrial processes, but the most common HFCS are 55% fructose and 45% glucose. Although it has not been proven that high fructose corn syrup causes type 2 diabetes, people in countries with higher availability of HFCS have a higher prevalence of type 2 diabetes independent of obesity,[2] high fruc-

---

2. Sigala, et al. "Dose-Response Effects," 1648.

tose corn syrup is thought to increase insulin resistance which is the primary cause of type 2 diabetes[3]. Humans enjoy sweets but sugar-rich foods should be consumed in moderation. Honey is a sugar solution comprised of about 40% fructose and 30% glucose, whereas maple syrup is primarily sucrose. Sugar (usually HFCS) is added to many foods, such as peanut butter, milk alternatives, ketchup, sauces, breads, dried fruits, etc. Sugars are not essential to our diet, so sugars are not needed for good health. Glucose can be made from amino acids or fats via a metabolic process called gluconeogenesis. Food labels list the contents in the package, from the most prevalent ingredients by weight to the least prevalent. Nutrition information includes serving size, calories, fat, saturated fat, trans fat, cholesterol, sodium, carbohydrates, fiber, sugar, protein, and vitamins and minerals, so read the labels to see what you are eating.

Fats

We humans need only two fatty acids that we cannot make. These essential fats are omega-3 fatty acids and omega-6 fatty acids. Good sources of omega-3 fatty acids are fatty fish such as salmon, mackerel, tuna, sardines, and herring, as well as flaxseed, chia seeds, and walnuts. Most Western diets contain more omega-6 fatty acids than we need because they are in vegetable oils such as soybean oil, corn oil, sunflower oil, and processed foods. Having a 1:4 ratio of omega-3 to omega-6 fatty acids reduces inflammation and promotes health. Improving the balance between the two essential fatty acids requires increasing omega-3 fatty acids in our diets by eating more fatty fish and/or by taking fish oil supplements, as well as eating flaxseeds and walnuts. And we also need to reduce processed and fried foods in our diets. Our cell membranes need omega fatty acids for hormone synthesis and brain development as well as other cellular functions. Olive oil, a staple of the Mediterranean diet, is rich in monounsaturated fats, which help lower bad

---

3. Goran, et al. "High Fructose Corn Syrup," 55–64.

cholesterol (LDL) and raise good cholesterol (HDL). Oleic acid is the major fatty acid in olive oil and is sometimes referred to as an omega-9 fatty acid, but it is not essential.

The Importance of Diet

The prophet Daniel refused the rich food and wine of Babylonian King Nebuchadnezzar and he asked for a test to compare diets. *"Please test your servants for ten days: Give us nothing but vegetables to eat and water to drink. Then compare our appearance with that of the young men who eat the royal food, and treat your servants in accordance with what you see." So he agreed to this and tested them for ten days. At the end of the ten days, they looked healthier and better nourished than any of the young men who ate the royal food. So the guard took away their choice food and the wine they were to drink and gave them vegetables instead."* (Daniel 1:12–16, NIV) The US FDA recommends a diet with more than 50% vegetables, whole grains, and fruits, along with lean meats, low-fat dairy, and foods rich in essential fatty acids (olive oil, avocado oil, and nuts).

Water, Oxygen, and Vitamins

The human body is about 60% water, and all our metabolic processes occur in aqueous solutions. We can live only a few days without water, and it is needed to flush out the waste products of metabolism, such as urea. Water, essential to life, is beautiful in the simplicity of its chemical structure, which will be presented later. Oxygen is brought into the body by hemoglobin in our red blood cells. Hemoglobin has four protein chains that like a four-passenger car, carry oxygen from our lungs to all our cells. Oxygen allows us to squeeze more energy from the foods we eat and keeps muscles working. Just as a fire will not burn without oxygen, our bodies need oxygen to metabolize our foods to CO_2 and water. Vitamins add chemical functions to many enzymes allowing them to catalyze reactions that would not be possible with just amino acids. Enzymes, the chemical factories of the body, process our foods and many of them need the vitamins in our diet to do their work. Drugs often work by inhibiting enzymes much like blocking the doors to certain metabolic factories.

Food is vital to life and mealtimes are spiritually important times to share our lives with friends and family. Food preparation is a time to work together for the benefit of others, as well as us. We all enjoy food and fellowship. Biblical references in Leviticus 11 and Deuteronomy 14 refer to certain animals that were "unclean" and should not be eaten. There are also references to not touching dead animals. We now know that some animals carry diseases that others do not. For example, pigs carry trichinosis, a roundworm parasite that infects muscles including the heart. Fortunately, cleaner farming practices and meat processing and cooking have greatly reduced infections. Biblical restrictions about not eating birds and other animals that eat dead or rotten flesh would have reduced exposure to bacteria and parasites. There are also numerous Biblical references to separating foods and washing which would have reduced the transmission of disease.

Holy Communion or the Eucharist

Holy Communion is a time to reflect on our lives and God's gift of grace and to remember the sacrifice of Christ Jesus for the forgiveness of our sins. It is spiritual nourishment, and a source of strength, forgiveness, and hope. For Catholics, the bread and wine are transformed into the body and blood of Christ, a mystical process known as transubstantiation. *"While they were eating, Jesus took bread, and when he had given thanks, he broke it and gave it to his disciples, saying, "Take and eat; this is my body." Then he took a cup, and when he had given thanks, he gave it to them, saying, "Drink from it, all of you. This is my blood of the covenant, which is poured out for many for the forgiveness of sins."* (Matthew 26:26–28, NIV). Consuming the bread and wine or fruit of the vine is a symbolic act of becoming one with Christ and fellow believers. *Jesus declared, "I am the bread of life. Whoever comes to me will never go hungry, and whoever believes in me will never be thirsty."* (John 6:35, NIV). The Communion service strengthens unity within the Christian community, and it is a time of personal renewal or re-commitment. Biochemically, the bread and wine are metabolized into molecules that become elements of our bodies (DNA and proteins), so Christ abides both spiritually and physically within Christians.

CHAPTER 3

Water and Hydrogen Bonds

"Water is life's matter and matrix, mother and medium. There is no life without water."

—ALBERT SZENT-GYORGYI, HUNGARIAN BIOCHEMIST, AND NOBEL LAUREATE[1]

God Makes the Weak and Insignificant Important

THE BIBLE CONTAINS NUMEROUS examples of God using weak or insignificant people to do miraculous things. Classic examples are Moses who stuttered, Jesus who was born in a stable and came from a tiny village, and most of Jesus' disciples who were uneducated men. *"But God chose the foolish things of the world to shame the wise; God chose the weak things of the world to shame the strong. God chose the lowly things of this world and the despised things—and the things that are not—to nullify the things that are, so that no one may boast before him."* (1 Corinthians 1:27–29, NIV) Simple water or H_2O is the most important molecule on earth. Water is the essence of life and so important that NASA scientists look first for water on other planets and moons as an indication that these

---

1. Szent-Gyorgyi, "Water is life's matter."

Water and Hydrogen Bonds

might have some life form. The human body is about 60% water, and we can only live without water for about three days, whereas we can survive about three weeks without food. Water molecules are composed of one oxygen atom and two hydrogen atoms, with each of the hydrogens linked to the oxygen via a strong covalent bond that involves the sharing of electrons between the two atoms. The unique beauty of water is in how the hydrogens are attached at an angle. This angularity results in the oxygen atom having a partial negative charge and the hydrogen atoms having a partial positive charge. Those slight charges allow water molecules to hydrogen bond to one another. Hydrogen bonds (H-bonds) are weak electrostatic attractions between polar molecules that are only 5–10% as strong as a covalent bond. H-bonds between water molecules create a three-dimensional network of molecules that is responsible for the cohesive forces that hold water together as a liquid and as ice crystals. If water did not have hydrogen bonds, it would boil at the frigid temperature of approximately -100 degrees C (-148 degrees F). Water is also the "universal solvent" because of the slight charges on the oxygen and hydrogens. Water is critical to the solubility of proteins in our blood and water aids the functions of other molecules, such as DNA. H-bonds give water its high surface tension and capillary forces that allow water to move up narrow tubes against the force of gravity used by all plants, such as trees and grass. The creation of water as a simple angular molecule with the ability to hydrogen bond to itself and other molecules was critical to life. *"But he said to me, "My grace is sufficient for you, for my power is made perfect in weakness." Therefore I will boast all the more gladly about my weaknesses, so that Christ's power may rest on me."* (2 Corinthians 12:9, NIV). As you will see later, God also used weak H-bonds to hold DNA strands together, and the realization of that simple fact was a major leap in Watson and Crick's discovery of the structure of the DNA double helix[2].

---

2. Watson and Crick, "Molecular Structure of Nucleic Acids."

Water

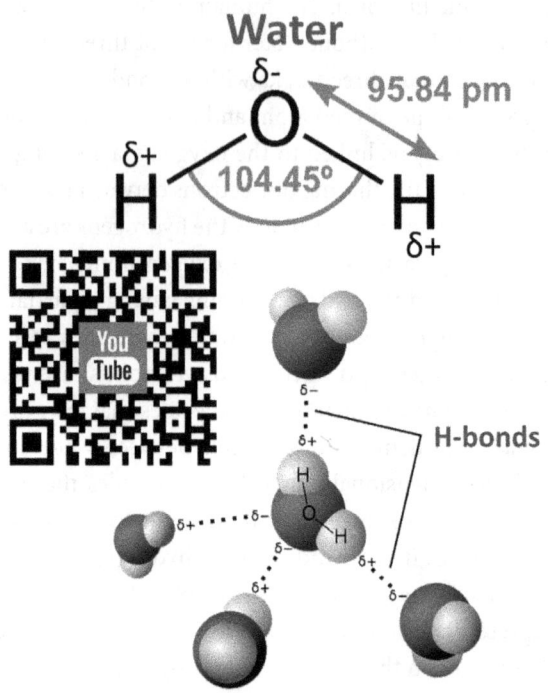

CHAPTER 4

The Facts of Life

"DNA: The Secret of Life"
—JAMES D. WATSON AND ANDREW BERRY[1]

The Genetic Alphabet and Words of Life

DNA (DEOXYRIBONUCLEIC ACID) HAS a simple composition of four nucleic acid bases, abbreviated with four letters, **A, T, G, and C**. This is the alphabet of life. You do not need to know anything about their chemical structures or chemical names, but that information is presented subsequently for those interested. DNA is a double helix held together by weak hydrogen bonds like those that hold water molecules together. DNA sequences tell the machinery of our cells which amino acids to link together and in what order to arrange the amino acids to make different proteins. DNA sequences are converted into RNA (ribonucleic acid) in a process known as transcription with three letters of RNA sequences being read by our cellular protein synthesis machine (called a ribosome) to determine which of the twenty amino acids to link together to make a particular protein. The sequences of amino acids are like

---

1. Watson and Berry, *"DNA: Secret of Life."*

words in sentences with different sequences making up different proteins. Amino acids also have chemical names given by their discoverers or based on their chemical properties. For simplicity we use single letters to denote each amino acid; **G, A, V, L, S, I, T, M, P, D, N, E, Q, H, K, R, C, F, Y, W.** There is no reason to memorize these letters or to know anything about their chemistry, that is what biochemists do. We also use three-letter abbreviations of the amino acids based on their chemical names. Unfortunately, some amino acids were given names with the same first letter so different single letters had to be used for them. Their names and single letter abbreviations are Glycine-G, Alanine-A, Valine-V, Leucine-L, Serine-S, Isoleucine-I, Threonine-T, Methionine-M, Proline-P, Aspartic Acid -D, Asparagine-N, Glutamic Acid-E, Glutamine-Q, Histidine-H, Lysine-K, Arginine-R, Cysteine-C, Phenylalanine-F, Tyrosine-Y, and Tryptophan-W.

DNA

The information that makes each organism different is encoded in its DNA and viewed as the alphabet of life. DNA is converted (transcribed) into messenger RNA (mRNA) in the nucleolus and the mRNA is moved to the cytoplasm of the cell where it is translated into proteins, such as bone collagen, hemoglobin, and enzymes. The protein synthesis machinery of the cell (ribosome) reads mRNA sequences three letters at a time to connect amino acids into different sequences. One can view amino acids a of the words of life and their sequences in different proteins akin to different sentences that convey different thoughts. For example, the sequence of insulin is different from hemoglobin, and enzymes needed for DNA replication are different from enzymes that convert proteins, fats, and sugars into energy.

All living things on earth use the same four nucleic acids or nucleotide bases as their genetic material and the same twenty amino acids are the building blocks of the enzymes and other proteins that do the work required by all cells to grow and replicate. There is one more amino acid called selenocysteine that has selenium in place of the sulfur in cysteine, but it is not directly coded for in DNA as the other 20 amino acids are, and it has been found in only 25 proteins. DNA is a double-stranded helix and every A in one strand pairs with a T in the opposite strand and they are held together by two hydrogen bonds (H-bonds). Likewise, every G is paired with a C and held together by three hydrogen bonds. Hydrogen bonds are very weak, but the double helix is stabilized by thousands or millions of H-bonds depending on the length of DNA. There is no need to memorize these structures or names, but to help you remember **AT** think **A**ppalachian **T**rail, and for **GC** think **G**ulf **C**oast.

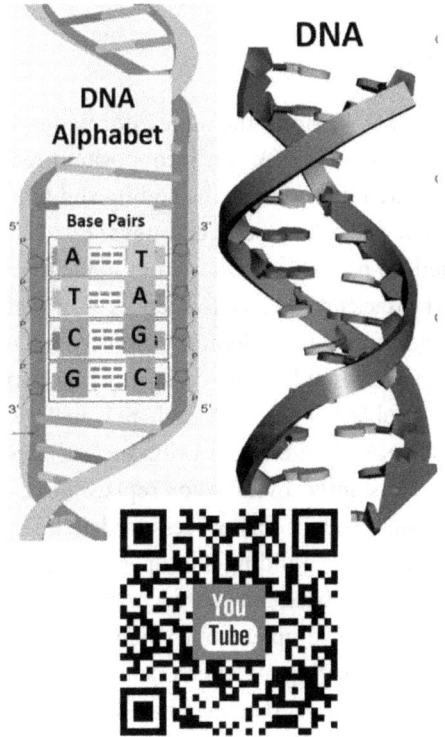

DNA polymers are exceptionally large molecules with each chromosome made of millions of base pairs. DNA nucleotide polymers (long sequences of molecules like plastic polymers) are linked by deoxyribose sugars and phosphate groups and the two polymer strands run in opposite directions, so they are said to be anti-parallel. The negatively charged phosphate linkage makes the molecule an acid. The deoxyribose in DNA makes it more stable than the ribose linkages in RNA. Only about 2% of our DNA codes for proteins and some of the non-coding DNA sequences control gene expression allowing cells to have distinct functions via the production of different proteins. For example, osteoblast cells produce collagen, a structural protein, whereas the beta cells of the pancreas make insulin. Beta cells do not make collagen and osteoblasts do not make insulin.

DNA Replication

Double-stranded DNA stores the same information in each strand and the two strands of DNA run in opposite directions to each other and they are referred to as the coding and template strands. Some cells, such as heart muscle cells, never divide after the heart is fully formed, so new heart cells are not made to repair injuries, such as heart attacks. Other cells such as skin cells, and blood stem cells divide frequently. Upon division (called mitosis) DNA strands are separated and a new complementary strand is made forming two double helixes with each new cell getting one old and one new DNA strand. Some cells, such as those lining our intestines are constantly dividing for replacement. Several good videos on the web explain this process in detail. DNA sequences are the instructions for building and operating an organism, and a damaged nucleotide base can cause a misreading of the instructions. Fortunately, the complementary nature of the DNA strands protects us from damaging mutagens, such as UV light, radiation, or mutagenic chemicals. A damaged base in a DNA sequence can be removed and replaced with the correct base that pairs with the correct undamaged base on the undamaged strand. This DNA repair process protects us and other organisms from mutations that can allow cells to become cancerous. Most cancers result from multiple mutations that accumulate with aging and failures in the repair processes. Basal cell skin cancers are common in older people. Mutations can also be beneficial, such as a frog with a longer tongue for catching insects, or a basketball player who can jump higher.

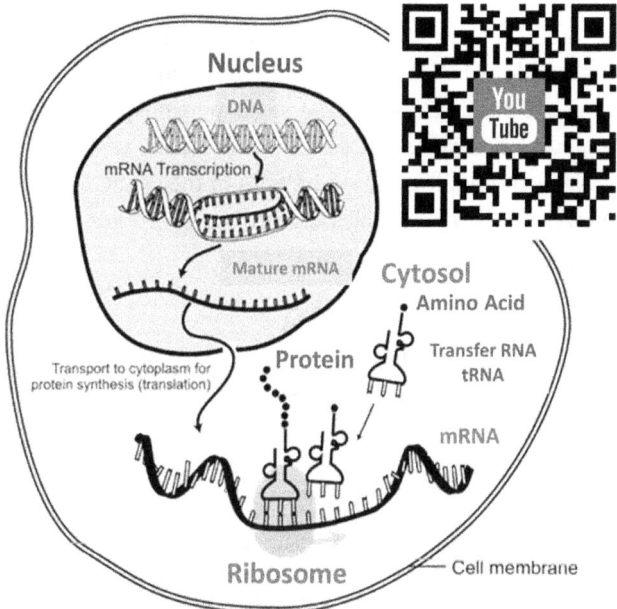

DNA Transcription into mRNA and mRNA Translation into Proteins (Sentences) - strings of Amino Acids

DNA is transcribed into messenger RNA (mRNA) in the nucleus, and then the mRNA enters the cytosol where it is translated by ribosomes (machinery) into proteins. Transfer RNAs (tRNAs) carry amino acids to the ribosome which strings them together.

Translation of DNA into the Protein Sentences of Life

Proteins are amino acids linked together in long chains: the sentences of life. An RNA polymerase binds to DNA and the template strand, converting the sequence into Messenger RNA (mRNA). Since it is made complementary to the non-coding or template strand of DNA, mRNA has the exact sequence of the DNA coding strand but with the letter U (uracil) in the place of T (thymine) as in DNA. The message encoded in messenger RNA (mRNA) moves from the nucleus to the cytosol of the cell where it turns into proteins (various amino acid sequences) using molecular machinery, called ribosomes. Transfer RNAs (tRNAs) carry the different amino acids to the ribosome which strings them together. RNA is not as stable as DNA because, without a complementary strand, repair is not possible. The ribose sugar-phosphate links between RNA nucleotides make RNA more fragile than DNA. Additionally, RNA is more difficult to work with in the lab because numerous enzymes called ribonucleases, found even on our fingers, that break down RNA.

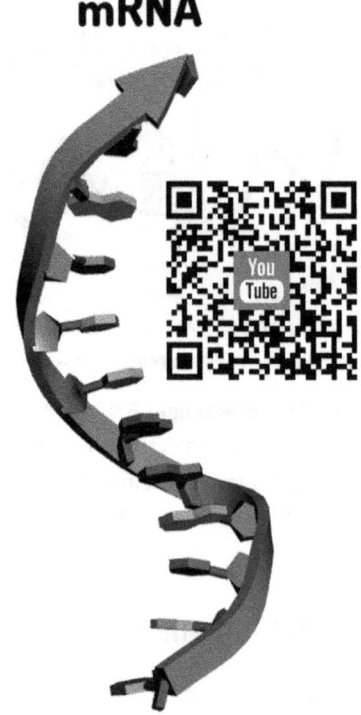

**Single nucleotide strand
A, U, G & C nucleotides
Less stable than DNA**

Genetic Code

The genetic code is universal: the same three bases code for the same amino acids in all organisms. The table below shows the DNA bases coding for the various amino acids. This table is color-coded to show the chemical similarities of the amino acids. Codons are the three bases that are read by the ribosome that code for each amino acid. There is more than one codon for most amino acids, except for Met and Trp. This redundancy means that mutations in the DNA often result in the same amino acid in the protein, even though the DNA code is slightly different. For example: TTT and TTC code for Phe, so a T to C or C to T mutation in the third position yields Phe. Amino acids with similar chemical structures have similar codes. Another example: All the red amino acids are somewhat hydrophobic (water repelling), so a mutation in the second or third position will result in a similar amino acid, such as Val in place of Leu. Ser and Thr have hydroxyl groups (OH) and they differ only in the first nucleotide base (A or T). Consequently, mutations in our genes often result in the same or a chemically similar amino acid in the resulting protein. Such mutations can be subtle with little effect on protein structure or function unless they occur in a critical location, such as the catalytic site of an enzyme or at some other important location.

The Genetic Code

	T	C	A	G	
T	Phe	Ser	Tyr	Cys	T
	Phe	Ser	Tyr	Cys	C
	Leu	Ser	STOP	STOP	A
	Leu	Ser	STOP	Trp	G
C	Leu	Pro	His	Arg	T
	Leu	Pro	His	Arg	C
	Leu	Pro	Gln	Arg	A
	Leu	Pro	Gln	Arg	G
A	Ile	Thr	Asn	Ser	T
	Ile	Thr	Asn	Ser	C
	Ile	Thr	Lys	Arg	A
	Met	Thr	Lys	Arg	G
G	Val	Ala	Asp	Gly	T
	Val	Ala	Asp	Gly	C
	Val	Ala	Glu	Gly	A
	Val	Ala	Glu	Gly	G

Universal Codon Table
T in DNA is replaced by U in RNA (DAJ)

Mitochondrial DNA

Our cells contain mitochondria which are organelles within cells that allow us to oxidatively metabolize carbon compounds, such as sugars. This gives us much more energy from our food sources, including proteins and sugars. Adenosine triphosphate (ATP) is the universal energy source of our bodies, used by enzymes to drive thermodynamically unfavorable reactions. Glycolysis is the process by which the body converts glucose and other sugars into ATP, which is needed, so our muscles can move, and it is used in making other molecules, such as amino acids and hormones. Glycolysis by itself makes only two ATP molecules per glucose molecule, but our mitochondria use oxygen to convert glycolysis by-products to CO_2 and water while making 36 ATP molecules per glucose molecule. Mitochondrial DNA codes for thirteen important proteins needed for the oxidative phosphorylation process that produces ATP while converting the sugars, proteins, and fats we eat into CO_2 and water, which are easily removed waste products. Only our mother's egg cells contain mitochondria, whereas sperm cells have no mitochondria. Consequently, we get more DNA from our mothers than our fathers and our moms give us our cellular energy factories. Muscle is rich in mitochondria and the number increases with exercise, especially with endurance training. Mutations in mitochondrial DNA can result in less active proteins and thus reduce energy production. Mutations can result spontaneously or be inherited. Some studies have found that the mitochondria of elite athletes are more efficient at producing energy (ATP) and that their mitochondria are more resistant to damage, but mitochondria are not the only factor.

CHAPTER 5

Proteins—the Sentences of Life

"Genes are effectively one-dimensional. If you write down the sequence of A, C, G and T, that's kind of what you need to know about that gene. But proteins are three-dimensional. They have to be because we are three-dimensional, and we're made of those proteins. Otherwise we'd all sort of be linear, unimaginably weird creatures."

—FRANCIS COLLINS[1]

Proteins Overview

PROTEINS ARE POLYMERS FOR amino acids that are connected like the beads of a necklace. By convention, protein sequences are numbered from amino acid number 1 at the amino terminus (NH_2+) to their carboxy terminus (CO_2-). Hemoglobin alpha chains have 141 amino acids, whereas beta chains have 146, and each has a different composition of amino acids and different sequences. The links between the amino acids are called peptide bonds. Proteins have different amino acid compositions. Casein, the major protein in milk, has an amino acid composition with adequate amounts

---

1 Collins, "Genes are effectively."

of the amino acids needed by infants or young calves for normal growth and development. Of the twenty amino acids, eleven can be made from non-protein food sources and these are called the non-essential amino acids because we do not need to eat them or eat proteins containing them, although we often do. The other nine amino acids must be in the plant or animal protein sources we eat, and they are called essential amino acids because we cannot make them from other foods. Later we will discuss this idea in more detail concerning foods rich in essential amino acids. Gelatin, which is made from the collagen in pigs' feet is not a good dietary source of protein because it is primarily comprised of the non-essential amino acids, glycine, and proline.

Protein - Polymer of Amino Acids

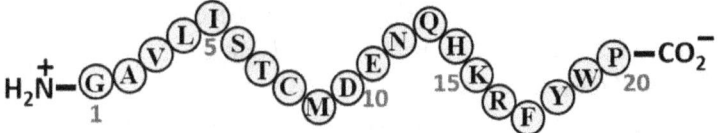

Amino Acid Single Letter Abbreviations

G-Glycine	S-Serine	E-Glutamic Acid	R-Arginine
A-Alanine	T-Threonine	N-Asparagine	F-Phenylalanine
V-Valine	C-Cysteine	Q-Glutamine	Y-Tyrosine
L-Leucine	M-Methionine	H-Histidine	W-Tryptophan
I-Isoleucine	D-Aspartic Acid	K-Lysine	P-Proline

All Life is Made of Proteins

Proteins are essential for life on Earth because they are the building blocks of all living cells, and they play a role in virtually every biological process. Structural proteins include collagen of bone, and keratin that makes up hair and nails. Actin and myosin are proteins needed for muscle contraction. Hemoglobin transports oxygen and myoglobin stores oxygen. Thousands of different enzymes, such as trypsin, speed chemical reactions, each with a specific function. Antibodies bind to invading bacteria and viruses to aid their killing. Our glands make numerous hormone proteins, and the bloodstream transports them to regulate growth, development, and reproduction. You do not need to know about all the proteins of the body to appreciate their importance to life. During Biblical times junk food and refined sugar were not available, yet the Bible refers to what we eat and drink to nurture our bodies. *"Do you not know that your bodies are temples of the Holy Spirit, who is in you, whom you have received from God? You are not your own."* (1 Corinthians 6:19, NIV). *"Therefore, I tell you, do not worry about your life, what you will eat or drink; or about your body, what you will wear. Is not life more than food, and the body more than clothes?"* (Matthew 6:25, NIV).

Only about 1–2% of human DNA codes for the approximately 25,000 proteins that make up our bodies, the rest of our DNA has other functions, such as regulating gene expression, protecting DNA from damage, and aiding DNA repair. We once referred to the non-coding regions as "junk DNA," but we continue to discover new roles for "junk DNA". Proteins fold into different and elegant 3D structures such as hemoglobin that transports oxygen from our lungs to all our cells. The most abundant human protein is the collagen of our bones, and other collagens give strength and form to other structures and tissues. Bone collagen is made of three proteins of about 1,000 amino acids each twisted much like a three-stranded rope and that makes it very strong. Collagen is the Holy Trinity of our bodies, like the Father, Son, and Holy Spirit. Other proteins include enzymes, such as trypsin that cut up dietary proteins so the amino acids can enter our blood to make body proteins, such as muscle and hemoglobin, as well as for our hair, skin, and eyes.

Linus Pauling discovered the alpha helix structure found in proteins in 1948 and Watson and Crick discovered the double

Proteins—The Sentences of Life

helical structure of DNA in 1953 using X-ray diffraction to determine the positions of atoms in 3D space. Both the alpha helix and double helix structures depend on hydrogen bonds. These advances were based on the work of numerous other scientists, as is always the case. The complete picture of a molecule or chemical process never results from a single experiment and usually involves multiple scientists working in different labs, sometimes on opposite sides of the globe.

The chemistry of biological molecules was far more mysterious and attractive to me than other areas of chemistry. To study a molecule, such as an enzyme or other protein, it has to be purified to separate it from all other molecules. This work was a major thrust of biochemistry in my early years, and I became interested in understanding how defective proteins could result in diseases. Such work also involved amino acid analysis and protein sequencing to determine the order in which amino acids were arranged for their unique sequences. Once we understood that three DNA bases coded for each amino acid, the sequencing of DNA quickly replaced the slow process of sequencing proteins. The sequence of the human genome completed in 2000, was a major leap forward because the sequence of most human proteins became evident. Then came developments allowing the production of human proteins in bacterial and yeast cells by inserting human DNA sequences. These so-called recombinant proteins were easy to purify, and we even made improved enzyme mutants by changing the DNA sequences used. Recombinant human insulins are now used in treating diabetes, which are much better than the original insulins isolated from a cow or pig pancreas. Insulin was discovered 100 years ago, and animal insulin proteins were used until recombinant human insulins became available in 1982. These are much better because they are identical to our normal human insulin, whereas animal insulins have slightly different amino acid sequences, which can cause some immunological complications. Slight changes in the amino acid sequences of recombinant insulin have resulted in slow-acting and fast-acting forms that physicians use to manage diabetic patients' blood sugar levels.

Different muscles in the body have different troponins that function in muscle contraction. Below is a figure showing multiple sequence alignment of three human muscle troponin proteins made in cardiac (heart) muscle, fast-twitch skeletal muscle, and slow-twitch skeletal muscle. Although their roles in muscle contraction are similar, their amino acid sequences are different, giving them different structures and somewhat different abilities. Percent identity was calculated relative to cardiac troponin, thus 57% of the amino acids in fast troponin are identical to those in cardiac, and 63% of the amino acids in slow troponin are identical to those in cardiac. The different colors aid in the comparison of the amino acid sequences and the colors are also related to similarities in chemical properties. Sequences are always written from the amino terminus to the carboxyl terminus. The long sequence of amino acids at the beginning of the cardiac sequence is not in the other two. This and other differences made possible simple antibody-based tests to measure cardiac troponin in the blood that is only present if the heart has been damaged. When patients arrive at the hospital emergency department complaining of chest pain, the staff will measure the patient's cardiac troponin levels to see whether they are having a heart attack or some other chest pain issue. This has led to many lives being saved.

Human Troponin I Sequence Alignment
Cardiac- cardiac muscle
Fast – fast skeletal muscle
Slow – slow skeletal muscle

```
Cardiac   MADGSSDAAREPRPAPAPIRRRSSNYRAYATEPHAKKKSKISASRKLQLKTLLLQIAKQE
Fast      ------------------------------MGDEEKRNRAITARRQHLKSVMLQIAATE
Slow      ------------------------------MPEVERKPKITASRKLLLKSLMLAKAKEC

Cardiac   LEREAEERRGEKGRALSTRCQPLELAGLGFAELQDLCRQLHARVDKVDEERYDIEAKVTK
Fast      LEKEESRREAEKQNYLAEHCPPLHIPG-SMSEVQELCKQLHAKIDAAEEEKYDMEVRVQK
Slow      WEQEHEEREAEKVRYLAERIPTLQTRGLSLSALQDLCRELHAKVEVVDEERYDIEAKCLH

Cardiac   NITEIADLTQKIFDLRGKFKRPTLRRVRISADAMMQALLGARAKESLDLRAHLKQVKKED
Fast      TSKELEDMNQKLFDLRGKFKRPPLRRVRMSADAMLKALLGSKHKVCMDLRANLKQVKKED
Slow      NTREIKDLKLKVMDLRGKFKRPPLRRVRVSADAMLRALLGSKHKVSMDLRANLKSVKKED
                                                    Percent Identity
Cardiac   TEKEN--REVGDWRKNIDALSGMEGRKKKFES-------  100%
Fast      TEKERDLRDVGDWRKNIEEKSGMEGRKKMFESES-----   57%
Slow      TEKERP-VEVGDWRKNVEAMSGMEGRKKMFDAAKSPTSQ   63%
```

Proteins—The Sentences of Life

Protein Structures

Biochemists have used X-ray diffraction of crystalized proteins to provide 3D structures of proteins. This technical process is somewhat like X-rays used to see broken bones, in which atomic nuclei cause the X-rays to scatter in such a way that their size and position in the crystal can be calculated. An X-ray photo and an understanding of hydrogen bonds helped Watson and Crick conceive and build a physical model of the structure of DNA in 1953. Rosalind Franklin had made a high-quality X-ray photo of DNA that indicated a helix, and Maurice Wilkins, Franklin's research director and mentor, had shown the photo to Watson. Scientists often share unpublished data because we are more interested in knowledge than fame. Watson, Crick, and Wilkins won the 1962 Nobel Prize in Physiology or Medicine for the discovery of the structure of DNA. Franklin did not share in their Nobel Prize because winners must be living and unfortunately, she died of ovarian cancer in 1958 at age 37.

We can now see the intricate structures of proteins and DNA on computer screens, the artistry of which is as amazing as the mountains, a sunset, sea life, or the gorgeous complexity of a flower. Computer modeling has allowed scientists to design drugs that fit precisely into the targeted enzyme to jam up its works. Just as anatomy has allowed us to see and understand the organs of the body, seeing protein structures has aided the education of medical and graduate students by allowing them to see how these molecules function in the body and understand how drugs treat a host of medical conditions by binding to proteins. Viruses like HIV and COVID-19 use RNA as their genetic material to code for a single long protein that they produce by taking over the process of the cells they invade. This protein contains multiple regions that code for the viral coat proteins and enzymes needed to take over the functions of the cells it invades. Included in that long protein is a protease that cuts apart and frees the individual protein components so a new virion (a viral particle that can infect other cells) can assemble. The process is like building a house from a single long piece of wood in which the protease is the molecular saw that cuts out the pieces of wood for the walls, windows, and doors of the new viral particle. Inhibitor drugs of the viral protease "jam up" the molecular saw enzyme so it cannot cut out the pieces needed to make a new viral particle. Treatment for HIV AIDS improved significantly with the development of molecules that inhibit the HIV protease and these protease inhibitors are also the drugs used by Pfizer to make Paxlovid® for treating COVID-19.

CHAPTER 6

Three Important Proteins

"We have seen that each type of protein consists of a precise sequence of amino acids that allows it to fold up into a particular three-dimensional shape, or conformation. But proteins are not rigid lumps of material. They can have precisely engineered moving parts whose mechanical actions are coupled to chemical events. It is this coupling of chemistry and movement that gives proteins the extraordinary capabilities that underlie the dynamic processes in living cells."

—BRUCE ALBERTS, AMERICAN BIOCHEMIST AND PRESIDENT OF THE NATIONAL ACADEMY OF SCIENCES[1]

Hemoglobin, Trypsin, and Collagen

PROTEINS COME IN VARIOUS shapes and sizes that perform different functions determined by their amino acid sequences or how the amino acid "words" are put together. Thousands of proteins work together so the body can function. Even the best biochemistry texts do not attempt to cover all these proteins, so we will look at only three different proteins and their functions. They are hemoglobin (oxygen transport), trypsin (an enzyme), and collagen

---

1. Alberts et al. *"Molecular Biology".*

(structural). As previously mentioned, our red blood cells (RBCs) are filled with hemoglobin which is responsible for their color. Hemoglobin transports oxygen from our lungs to our tissues through our arteries. Every second about two million new RBCs emerge from our bone marrow to replace the two million old RBCs that die every second. Each RBC contains about 250 million molecules of hemoglobin. Our miraculous bodies are making about 500 quintillion molecules of new hemoglobin every second, which is equivalent to the number of seconds in 16 billion years. We need oxygen to oxidize the fuels we eat to carbon dioxide (CO_2) and water to get the maximum amount of energy from our foods so our muscles and organs can work properly. Oxygen allows us to get 17 times more energy from each molecule of glucose than via glycolysis alone. RBCs also help remove carbon dioxide, a waste product of metabolism, from our bodies and that role will be discussed later.

The chemical reactions of the body are rapidly catalyzed by metabolic enzymes to produce enough energy for us to move quickly. Enzymes are catalysts that speed up chemical reactions by lowering the activation energy of chemical reactions. Activation energy is the minimum amount of energy that is needed for a reaction to occur. Over 7,000 enzymes in our bodies catalyze the metabolism of our foods to produce energy (ATP) and to synthesize a host of molecules such as hormones. Trypsin is a protease enzyme that cuts up proteins by breaking certain peptide bonds in the proteins we eat. It is one of the molecular saws referred to in the analogy of cutting up proteins (wooden boards) to make our bodies (our houses). Enzymes are also proteins comprised of hundreds to thousands of amino acids. Enzyme active sites usually involve only a few amino acids held in a special 3D arrangement that speeds up a particular chemical reaction, and the rest of the protein folds to position the active site amino acids just so. Several enzymes need more than just amino acids to catalyze some reactions and they employ additional organic molecules. Most of these added compounds are dietary vitamins or compounds made from vitamins. Trypsin does not need vitamins, but it is an excellent example of an enzyme.

Collagen is the most abundant protein in the body, and we have 28 different types of this structural protein. Type I, the most prevalent, is the starting material for our bones. It is comprised of three protein chains, each containing more than 1,000 amino acids that wrap around each other like a twisted three-strand rope. Other collagens also have some triple helical structure and other aspects that are needed in various tissues giving them structure and flexibility.

Twenty Amino Acid Words of Life
Three-Letter and Single-Letter
Abbreviations
Essentials are Green

```
Gly-Ala-Val-Leu-Ile
Ser-Thr-Cys-Met-Pro
Asp-Asn-Glu-Gln-Phe
Tyr-Trp-His-Lys-Arg


G-A-V-L-I-S-T-C-M-P
D-N-E-Q-F-Y-W-H-K-R
```

CHAPTER 7

Hemoglobin

"A discovery is like falling in love and reaching the top of a mountain after a hard climb all in one, an ecstasy not induced by drugs but by the revelation of a face of nature that no one has seen before and that often turns out to be more subtle and wonderful than anyone had imagined."

—MAX PERUTZ, NOBEL LAUREATE[1]

Hemoglobin Structure

HEMOGLOBIN IS COMPOSED OF four proteins, two alpha, and two beta subunits and each has a heme group with iron that binds oxygen. There are separate genes for each subunit. Heme is an organic molecule that contains iron, and it helps hemoglobin bind oxygen in the lungs and release oxygen in our tissues, such as our big toe. Other physiologically important aspects of this marvelous molecule have been determined through years of research and can be learned by searching the internet or by taking biochemistry or physiology courses.

1. Perutz, "Discovery is like."

Hemoglobin

Molecules, such as the red blood cell protein hemoglobin that carries oxygen from our lungs to all our tissues, are beautiful in their structure and function. Hemoglobin moves when it binds and releases oxygen. Like our lungs, it expands when we inhale, and it contracts when it releases oxygen that it has transported to the far regions of our bodies. It breathes when we breathe. Hemoglobin has four protein pieces, called subunits, which are held together by hydrogen bonds and other weak forces, but no covalent chemical bonds. Its two alpha subunits and two beta subunits differ a little in their amino acid sequences. They are also the same in that each has a heme group which is an organic molecule that binds an iron $Fe+2$ ion. In chemistry, we use letter symbols for chemicals such as Fe for iron, and then a number to tell us more. Each heme has an $Fe+2$ with two positive charges at its core, whereas $Fe+3$ has three positive charges. This $Fe+2$ ion allows hemoglobin to bind oxygen, whereas $Fe+3$ does not bind oxygen, and instead binds water, which happens when iron rusts. Iron is so important that we also have other proteins that bind and transport iron and store it until needed. The structure of hemoglobin was obtained via X-ray crystallography (a technique used to determine the structure of proteins and DNA) by Max Perutz at Cambridge. In 1985 I was on a three-month research stint at Strangeways Laboratory in Cambridge and had the pleasure of meeting Professor Perutz. This was such a major advance in the study of proteins that Perutz won a Nobel Prize. Perutz was an Austrian Jew who had been baptized Catholic before he went to England to study. When WWII started, the British government sent him to Newfoundland, Canada along with other persons of German or Austrian background who were possibly sympathetic to the Nazis or potential spies. After several months he returned to Cambridge to help the war effort. Before studying hemoglobin, Perutz had studied ice crystals in glaciers in Switzerland and he advised the military about hiding commandos in glaciers. Because of his pre-war research into the changes in the arrangement of the crystals in the layers of a glacier, he was asked for advice on whether a battalion of commandos might shelter under Norwegian glaciers. Due to the British secrecy about wartime exploits, we do not know whether his expertise helped the war effort, but it did bring Perutz back to Cambridge and allowed him to continue the study of crystals which led to the crystallization of hemoglobin for X-ray crystallography.

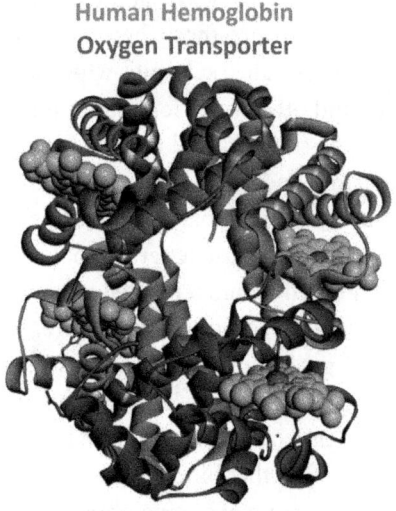

**Human Hemoglobin
Oxygen Transporter**

Red Alpha Subunits   Blue Beta Subunits
Green Hemes with Red Fe^{+2} Atoms

Heme, Lead Poisoning, Purple Urine, and Vampires

Without heme, hemoglobin would not transport oxygen, and heme is also used by proteins called cytochromes that are involved in other metabolic processes, such as the metabolism of drugs and other potentially harmful compounds. Heme is so important that there are multiple enzymes organized in what biochemists call a pathway to make it. Heme synthesis starts with two molecules that are easily made from glucose and other dietary molecules. The process starts in the mitochondria, the energy factory of cells, which will be discussed later. Glycine, the simplest amino acid, is one of the starting materials. Unfortunately, the heme synthesis process can be interrupted by lead poisoning and some genetic defects can reduce the synthesis of heme.

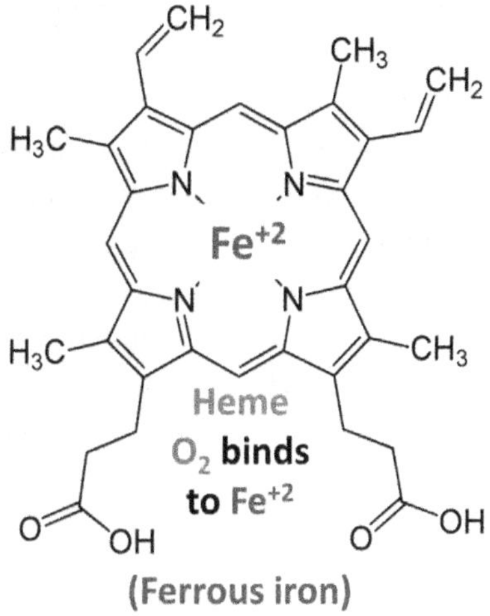

Heme
O_2 binds to Fe^{+2}
(Ferrous iron)

Lead poisoning causes developmental delays and anemia in children. When a child with anemia comes to a pediatrician, they will ask the parents about the age of their house because many old houses have lead-based paint that the child may have ingested. In 2015 lead was found in the Flint Michigan water. Until banned by the EPA, lead was used in gasoline to reduce engine "knock." Anemia is a major symptom of lead poisoning, but it also causes neurological damage.

Acute Intermittent porphyria is a genetic disease of heme synthesis resulting in acute attacks of gastrointestinal (stomach pain), neurologic/psychiatric, and cardiovascular symptoms. It is exacerbated by drugs and ethanol that require liver cytochromes for their metabolism. Hormonal changes can also initiate attacks. Porphyria is derived from porphyra a Greek word used to describe someone who is purple or in the case of Lydia whose conversion is recorded in Acts. 16:14 a dealer in purple cloth. The urine of those with this genetic condition turns purple after being exposed to light. Vincent van Gogh, the famous painter who cut off one of his ears, and Mad King George, of American Revolution times, are thought to have had acute intermittent porphyria.

Porphyria Cutanea Tarda is another heme synthesis defect that results in a heme-like compound in the skin that causes painful blisters when exposed to sunlight. Thus, those who suffer from this porphyria avoid being outdoors during the daytime. This heme-like metabolite also makes the teeth red. So, in more ancient times these poor souls with red teeth who came out at night to work, shop, or visit friends were thought to be vampires.

Sickle Cell Anemia

Sickle Cell Anemia causes red blood cells to clump together and get stuck in small blood vessels because Sickle Cell hemoglobin polymerizes when oxygen saturation drops. Normal red blood cells are oval discs that are very flexible, and they can squeeze through tiny capillaries because they lack a nucleus or mitochondria. Sickled red blood cells get stuck in capillaries and die, which results in tissue damage and pain. Sickle Cell hemoglobin beta subunits have a valine amino acid (uncharged and hydrophobic), whereas normal hemoglobin has glutamic acid amino acid (negatively charged and hydrophilic). People with Sickle Cell Disease, which is more prevalent in people with equatorial African ancestry, have shorter lives, suffer from severe pain (often requiring narcotics for relief) due to clogged blood vessels, and are prone to strokes and other complications. The Sickle Cell gene is most prevalent in malaria-endemic regions of Africa because those who are genetic carriers (heterozygous) of the gene are more resistant to the malaria parasite. Carriers do not have Sickle Cell Disease, but they can resist malaria because when red blood cells are infected by the parasite the cells sickle and die, also killing the parasite. Some sickle cell patients have been cured using gene therapy in which some of the patient's stem cells are removed from their bone marrow, followed by replacement with a normal beta subunit gene or mutation of the Sickle Cell gene to the normal sequence. It has long been known that infants who have Sickle Cell Disease do not suffer from sickled red crisis and pain because they still have fetal hemoglobin in which the hemoglobin beta chain lacks the disease mutation, and some people have milder disease because they continue to produce a little fetal hemoglobin as they get older. After we are born our fetal hemoglobin gene switches off and our adult hemoglobin beta gene turns on. Fetal hemoglobin aids the transfer of oxygen from the mother's hemoglobin to the fetus.

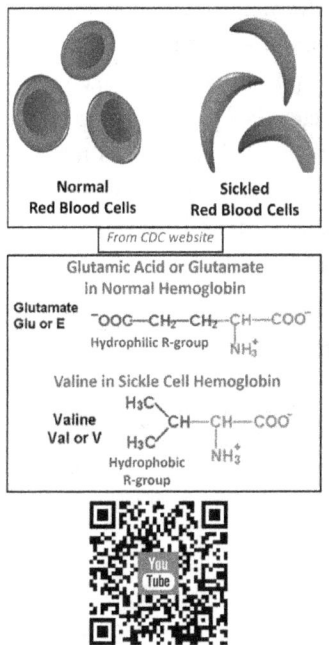

Blue People of Kentucky

A family in the Troublesome Creek community of eastern Kentucky in Appalachia was known as the Blue People. They had a recessive genetic deficiency in an enzyme that converts Fe^{+3} to Fe^{+2} in hemoglobin which resulted in homozygous individuals (two damaged genes) having blue lips, noses, ears, and fingers. This is an example of an interesting mutation that reduces the function of a protein. If the enzyme protein had been missing or totally inactive, the people would not have lived. Due to only a partial deletion of the enzyme, family members lived normal healthy lives, but some of them were shy or embarrassed by their blueness. They inherited a recessive gene that coded for a less than fully functional enzyme from early settlers in Troublesome Creek, Kentucky, near Hazzard[2]. Children who inherited two copies of the gene were blue, but the others were carriers. Troublesome Creek, like other communities in Appalachia, was isolated due to the lack of roads, bridges, and modes of transportation. With few outsiders coming in, there were marriages between cousins, and this resulted in some blue relatives. The defective gene has now been diluted to the point that it is unlikely that carriers will marry another carrier. Below is a genetic pedigree based on information about the Blue People. When cousins married, all children were either carriers or Blue. Also, note; that when carriers married non-carriers, the gene was diluted out resulting in only carriers and non-carriers of the partially defective gene.

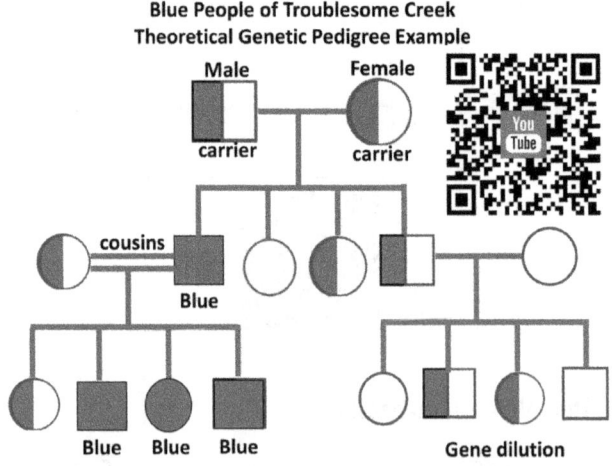

2. Cawein, et al. "Hereditary Diaphorase Deficiency" 578–85.

Hemoglobin and Jaundice

Red blood cells make up about 50% of our blood volume. Doctors frequently check hemoglobin levels because it is so important. Our bone marrow makes red blood cells, which live about 100–120 days. When red blood cells die the hemoglobin protein is broken into its amino acids which can be used to make new hemoglobin or other proteins. The organic heme molecule is changed into bilirubin yellow-orange colored pigment which is hydrophobic (water-hating), so it binds to hydrophobic amino acids on serum albumin. Albumin transports bilirubin to the liver where sugar molecules are attached to it to make it soluble. Then it is secreted via the gallbladder into the intestines where bacteria act on it to make our stools brown. A small amount is reabsorbed into the blood, goes to the kidneys, and makes urine yellow. Liver diseases often result in jaundice in which the whites of the eyes become yellow because a sick liver cannot make the heme soluble, and albumin can bind only so much bilirubin so the excess binds proteins throughout the body. The yellowing eyes and skin are most evident in lighter-skinned people. If you become dehydrated your urine becomes a darker yellow because it has a higher concentration of heme degradation products. Drinking more water is the usual remedy. Athletes and people working outdoors in hot weather must drink adequate water. Athletes who overwork their muscles can develop a condition called rhabdomyolysis in which damaged muscles release myoglobin which causes the urine to turn dark. There is more myoglobin in muscle than in most other cells because myoglobin stores oxygen needed for energy generation in the muscle. Myoglobin's small size causes it to get stuck in the kidneys and what passes through the kidneys results in brown "tea" colored urine, so there is the danger of kidney damage in rhabdomyolysis.

Hemoglobin A1c and Diabetes

What is hemoglobin A1c, and why should you want to know yours? It is easy for doctors to draw blood and check hemoglobin

A1c (or just "A1c") levels. This results in determining blood glucose (sugar) levels over three months. Just as candies stick to our fingers, sugars stick to the proteins in our bodies, but the sugars stuck to our proteins cannot be washed off because it is irreversible. Diabetes (Type 1 and Type 2) is due to high blood glucose levels and glucose attaches to many proteins which can result in blindness, kidney failure, and strokes. Measuring blood A1c levels tells doctors how well the various treatments for diabetes are working, because while glucose provides our body's energy, too much of this sugar damages the proteins it binds to. Since red blood cells live about three months our hemoglobin is replaced with new molecules every three months and A1c levels should go down to normal with the right medications, diet, and exercise.

We should note that our blood cells are comprised of components that are important in monitoring our health. Doctors get blood tests to see if we have infections, or malfunctions and use these tests to help diagnose illnesses such as anemia or leukemia. As a biochemist I and many others have gone deeper into trying to understand what makes these work at a cellular level so better treatments can be devised. When you see your blood test, you will see counts for WBC (white blood cells), RBC (red blood cells), platelets, and amounts of hemoglobin. When the doctor is concerned, further tests that look at other components can be ordered. Understanding the makeup, form, and function of blood cells is important and is an ongoing study. God's amazing and wonderful hand is evident in the smallest of cells. *"I praise you because I am fearfully and wonderfully made; your works are wonderful, I know that full well."* (Psalm 139:14, NIV).

CHAPTER 8

Enzymes

"Nature is solving all sorts of problems that we throw at her - how to degrade plastic bottles, how to degrade pesticides and herbicides and antibiotics. She creates new enzymes in response to that all the time, in real-time.".
—FRANCES ARNOLD, NOBEL PRIZE IN CHEMISTRY.[1]

Trypsin Example of an Enzyme

ENZYMES ARE CATALYSTS THAT speed up chemical reactions without themselves being changed and without the input of heat. Around 20,000 human genes encode enzymes, and variations that occur during the expression process are thought to produce over 50,000 unique proteins. Trypsin is a protease enzyme that cuts up (digests) the proteins we eat as part of our diets so the amino acids in food can be used to make new human proteins, such as muscle myosin and hemoglobin. Trypsin is a classic example of an enzyme, presented in every biochemistry textbook. As you can see from the picture below, it has a little red alpha helix, but most of its secondary structure is beta-sheets. The pancreas secretes it as trypsinogen, an inactive or zymogen form of trypsin, which

1. Arnold, "Nature is solving."

protects the pancreas. If trypsin was prematurely activated in the pancreas it would damage/irritate the pancreas, as happens with pancreatitis. Trypsinogen is secreted into the intestines where it is activated by intestinal enteropeptidase which cuts off a short segment of amino acids from its amino terminus. Trypsin then folds in a very precise way to create a chemical factory that is called an active site by bringing three amino acids (serine, histidine, and aspartic acid) together from far-reaching positions in the protein sequence to create a pocket where the chemistry of the enzymatic process occurs. Those three amino acids are precisely positioned so they can attack the peptide bonds (chemical bonds) in dietary proteins without damaging trypsin's protein structure. Trypsin cuts dietary proteins at the amino acids lysine and arginine, then other protease enzymes finish breaking the proteins into individual amino acids that can then enter the blood. Proteases that use serine in their active sites are called serine proteases. A host of similar serine proteases participate in processes such as bacterial killing and blood clotting. Blood clotting involves the activation of multiple zymogen proteases via limited proteolysis, much like enteropeptidase activation of trypsinogen. They too have a critical serine amino acid in their catalytic sites and fold like trypsin but with some differences in their amino acid sequences. The last clotting protease to be activated is thrombin which converts fibrinogen, a soluble blood protein into insoluble fibrin forming a mesh-like patch at the cut to stop bleeding. The various serine proteases seem to have evolved from an ancestral serine protease enzyme which may have served both digestive and coagulation functions. The separation of these functions over time probably led to the distinct enzymes we see today. This evolutionary process is much like the first car Ford made. Many other cars and trucks followed, all with internal combustion engines, yet they were also different in other ways. Neutrophils (white blood cells) have several serine proteases with varied functions that aid bacterial killing. Several years ago, I got a vanity car license plate that read TRYPSIN because much of my research has dealt with trypsin and trypsin inhibitors. You know what trypsin is, but others tried to add more letters to figure out its meaning. When my wife drove my car while hers was in the shop her co-workers laughed, and some people asked me if I was a urologist. They were reading TRYPSIN as TRY PISSIN', so I changed my license plate to BIOKMST.

The specificities of enzymes and their active sites make them good targets for drugs. Penicillin inhibits enzymes needed to synthesize the cell walls of gram-positive and some gram-negative bacteria, thus killing them. Our livers make about three times more cholesterol than we eat, and high levels of cholesterol in our blood can result in cholesterol-rich deposits called plaques that clog our arteries and can lead to heart attacks and strokes. Consequently, doctors often prescribe one of several drugs like Lipitor or Crestor (called statins) to block a liver enzyme that makes cholesterol to reduce the buildup of cholesterol-rich arterial plaques.

Human Trypsin
protein digestive enzyme

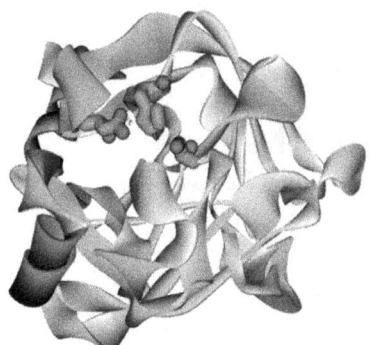

Red Alpha Helix
Blue Beta Sheet Ribbons

The Most Important Enzyme on Earth

Have you ever wondered how plants use sunlight to grow? The most important protein on earth is thought to be a plant enzyme called RuBisCo (Ribulose-1,5-bisphosphate carboxylase/oxygenase). In photosynthesis, chlorophyll (green) in plants harvests light energy from the sun to produce chemical energy that is used in the Calvin Cycle to make glucose (sugar). Water and carbon dioxide (CO_2) are consumed, and oxygen is produced along with glucose that the plant uses for energy and to make cellulose fibers for its structure. RuBisCo is in all photosynthetic organisms, including plants, algae, and some bacteria, playing a critical role in the Calvin Cycle. RuBisCo is comprised of eight large protein subunits of about 470 amino acids each along with eight magnesium ions and eight small subunits of about 175 amino acids each. Although some enzymes are amazingly fast, such as carbonic anhydrase in red blood cells which process 600,000 molecules of CO_2 per second, RuBisCo is slow, converting only 3–10 CO_2 molecules each second per molecule of enzyme. It is estimated that the total amount of RuBisCo on Earth is three hundred trillion tons, based on the assumption that the total amount of carbon fixed annually by RuBisCo is about 120 billion tons. Without RuBisCo there would be no life on earth because plants are at the bottom of the food chain. Chickens eat corn and insects, and we eat chicken which contains the same amino acids that our bodies need for growth and development. Fish feed on insects and smaller sea life, then little fish are eaten by bigger fish, and humans and bears eat salmon.

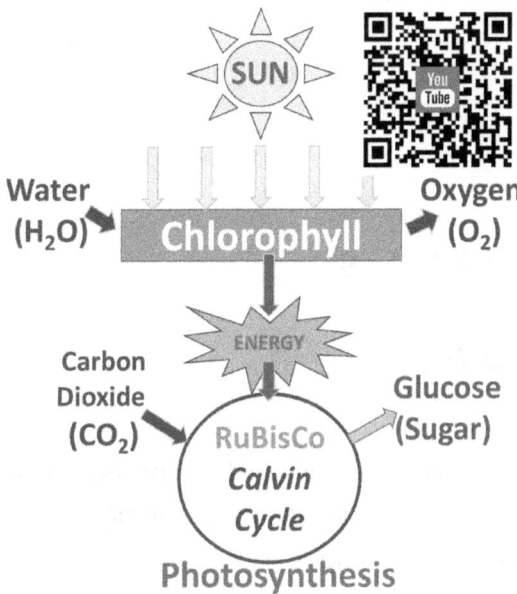

Photosynthesis

Our sun and all stars are enormous balls of hydrogen in which gravity forces the hydrogen atoms together under pressures so great that two hydrogen nuclei (single protons) merge and fuse to form a heavier helium nucleus. Energy is released when matter is lost due to two protons combining into a heavier helium nucleus, releasing a tremendous amount of energy according to Einstein's famous equation $E=mc^2$. The sun's core is about ten million degrees Celsius. Every second the sun produces the energy of approximately fifteen billion thermonuclear bombs. Only about 0.00000005% of that energy reaches Earth, of which the atmosphere absorbs 50% and reflects another 30% into space. This speaks to God's power as the creator of our sun and billions of even larger stars. Scientists have struggled to produce sustainable fusion reactions for energy production. If there were only a few stars, one might assume that they occurred by chance, but the vast number of these simple powerful fusion reactors throughout space provide evidence for a creator who used mind boggling powers and hydrogen, the smallest of atoms, to light up the night sky.

CHAPTER 9

Collagen

"Though one may be overpowered, two can defend themselves. A cord of three strands is not quickly broken."
(ECCLESIASTES 4:12, NIV)

Collagen the Structural Protein

COLLAGEN HAS A ROD-LIKE triple helical structure much like a three-strand rope. Bone collagen protein strands self-assemble with about a 1/3rd overlap somewhat like bricks in a wall. Once stacked the rods are cemented together by chemical bonds and calcium phosphate is added to produce solid bone. Depending on the burial conditions human skeletons can last anywhere from about 6 years to thousands of years. Christians believe that prophesy was fulfilled when Jesus's legs were not broken, which was often done to hasten the death of those being crucified. *"But when they came to Jesus and found that he was already dead, they did not break his legs."* (John 19:33, NIV), referring to *"he protects all his bones, not one of them will be broken."* (Psalms 34:20, NIV) and in preparing the Passover feast *"It must be eaten inside the house; take none of the meat outside the house. Do not break any of the bones."* (Exodus 12:46, NIV). Bone collagen has two virtually identical protein strands and the third is slightly different, so these could be viewed as the body's Holy Trinity, Father, Son, and Holy Spirit. A three-strand rope is strong, and before computers did graphics, I used a short piece of three-strand rope to show students how collagen strands were twisted.

**Three Proteins twisted
like a three-strand rope**

There are twenty-eight different collagens with different structural functions in the human body. All have triple helical sections, but bone collagen has the most. Approximately 67% of collagen is made of non-essential amino acids (glycine, proline, alanine, and hydroxyproline), which is important because we need to make a great deal of collagen. If collagen required very many essential amino acids, collagen production would be too dependent on diet. A diet with high-quality proteins (meat, milk, and eggs) provides the essential amino acids. Gelatin, which is made from collagen is not a good dietary protein because it lacks tryptophan and methionine, two essential amino acids needed to make proteins, such as muscle and hemoglobin.

Osteogenesis Imperfecta-Fragile Bones

A Viking King named Ivar the Boneless was supposedly carried into battle on his shield, and he is thought to have had Osteogenesis Imperfecta (OI). Every other amino acid in the collagen proteins is glycine because it is the smallest amino acid with only a hydrogen R-group, and this allows the three strands to tightly wrap together. Genetic mutations in collagen strands that replace glycine with larger amino acids interfere with the wrapping of the three protein strands needed for a strong triple helix, and this can result in fragile bones. OI can be more, or less severe, depending on the size of the amino acid that replaces glycine and on its position in the protein sequence. When a young French boy had this disease and could not run and play as most children do, his father built him a special piano bench so he could reach the keys. This boy went on to be an internationally famous jazz pianist. A former mayor and successful banker in a nearby city is wheelchair-bound by OI, but he is living a full and rewarding life. God works in mysterious ways.

Cartilage Cushions Joints

The cartilage which cushions our joints is comprised of collagen, proteoglycans containing glycosaminoglycan sugars, and chondroitin sulfate. Billions of dollars are spent yearly on glucosamine and chondroitin sulfate supplements to ease arthritis pain. However, a large NIH-supported study found that these supplements were no better than a placebo.[1] This result is logical because our

---

1. Clegg, et al. "Glucosamine, Chondroitin Sulfate."

digestive tract breaks down all proteins into amino acids and complex sugars into simple components for absorption through our intestinal epithelium; therefore, these supplements cannot reach our joints. Cartilage is made by chondrocytes which have the machinery for constructing and secreting cartilage, and they are slow growing which slows the healing of damaged cartilage. Additionally, the FDA does not analyze or test dietary supplements to see if they contain what they claim or have any benefit, but the FDA takes action when supplements are adulterated or misbranded. Read the labels.

Scurvy

Vitamin C is needed to convert proline amino acids in collagen to hydroxyproline which stabilizes the collagen triple helix. Great Britain in the 1700's was a powerful seafaring nation, but scurvy was a major problem. Commodore Anson set out to sail around the world in the 1740s with over 1,800 men, but after four years at sea he returned with only 188; most had died of scurvy. Vitamins had not yet been discovered and most physicians attributed the ravages of scurvy to bad drinking water, sea salt, or something in the air. Dr. James Lind, a Scottish physician, wrote in his 1757 "A Treatise on Scurvy",[2] that the sailors had black and blue spots all over their bodies, their gums became spongy and rotten with stinking breath, their legs were swollen with bleeding ulcers, they had universal cutaneous itchy eruptions and they tore their skin by scratching, they were in considerable pain, with shortness of breath and the numbers of deaths increased with time at sea. Their diet was primarily hard-tack biscuits, salt-cured meat, dried peas, cheese, and a gallon of beer a day. Lind thought acids in the diet might help but he had no proof, so he performed the first clinical trial while onboard a ship. Small groups of suffering sailors were given citrus fruits (oranges and lemons), cider, vinegar, seawater, a sulfuric acid mixture, or a medicinal purgative (laxative). Only

2. Lind, "Treatise on scurvy."

those receiving the citrus fruits improved. Unfortunately, the British Admiralty did not add limes to sailors' diets until 40 years later. Changing how people think about things they cannot see is a slow process, and politicians are often slow to act upon the science. It wasn't until 1928 that Hungarian biochemist Albert Szent-György isolated vitamin C^3, and it was 1962 before Drs. Irving Stone and Alton Meister discovered its role in stabilizing the structure of collagen[4].

3. Szent-Györgyi, "Observations," 1387–409.
4. Stone and Meister, "Function of ascorbic," 555–7.

CHAPTER 10

Blood- the Stream of Life

"All things are connected like the blood that unites us all. Man did not weave the web of life; he is merely a strand in it. Whatever he does to the web, he does to himself." Chief Seattle[1] *"The body is a community made up of its innumerable cells or inhabitants."*[2]

—THOMAS A. EDISON, INVENTOR

Blood Cells

BLOOD IS ESSENTIAL TO life and blood sacrifices to the gods were common in early cultures and some cultures even sacrificed humans. Abraham thought God wanted him to sacrifice his young son Isaac, but just as Abraham was about to kill Isaac with a knife, God stopped him and provided a ram (Genesis 22:12–13, NIV) to take Isaac's place on the altar. The Bible records many blood sacrifices of animals and of humans, such as by kings Ahaz (2 Chronicles 28:3, NIV) and Manasseh (2 Chronicles 33: 6, NIV) who both worshiped Ba'al, rather than the LORD God. "They

---

1. Seattle, "Chief Seattle's Speech".
2. Edison, "Body is a community."

sacrificed their sons and their daughters to false gods. They shed innocent blood, the blood of their sons and daughters, whom they sacrificed to the idols of Canaan, and the land was desecrated by their blood." (Psalms 106: 37–38, NIV). Blood is mentioned 369 times in the Bible and 170 times in the Qur'an. Christians partake of Holy Communion using bread representing the body of Christ broken for the redemption of our sins and wine or grape juice representing the blood of Christ shed for our redemption. Jesus was the perfect lamb of God sacrificed for the sins of all mankind. The Catholic Church holds that the bread and wine of the Eucharist, are changed into the body and blood of Christ upon consecration in the service, even though the bread and wine remain unchanged in their outward appearance, and looks, feels, and tastes like bread and wine. So, belief in transubstantiation is a matter of personal faith, as there is no scientific evidence to prove or disprove the doctrine.

Have you ever cut your finger and wondered what was in the blood? We each have about five liters of blood that flow through approximately 60,000 miles of arteries and veins. At a resting heart rate of sixty beats per minute, it takes only sixty seconds for blood to circulate throughout the body. Blood appears to be a liquid, but about 50% of it is cells, with the great majority being red blood cells that carry oxygen and about 1% white blood cells of several different types and functions. We have all heard the saying "blood is thicker than water" meaning that our family relationships are more important than other relationships, but blood is thicker than water due to the cells and proteins in it. The heart pumps oxygenated blood throughout the body and the veins are the return "plumbing" that takes it back to the lungs for reoxygenation.

Blood Cell Diversity

Blood cells are made in the bone marrow, and they all begin life as stem cells, just as we all begin life as infants. Like our growth and development into individuals, so do our blood cells grow and mature into different cell types. The adjacent picture shows the development of stem cells into most of our blood cells and each cell plays an important role in our bodies. Although all our blood cells are important in different ways, we will focus on only four major cell types because these are the most useful in understanding bodily functions and medical care.

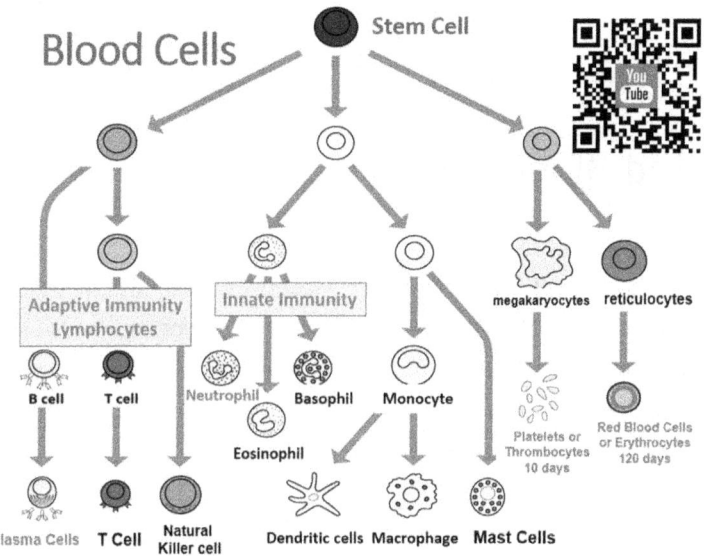

CHAPTER 11

Red Blood Cells

"The study of the red blood cells has always been and, without doubt, will continue to be one of the most important fields of investigation in general physiology..."

—KARL LANDSTEINER, AUSTRIAN BIOLOGIST
AND NOBEL LAUREATE[1]

Red Blood Cells

HAVE YOU EVER WONDERED why blood is red? Red blood (RBC) cells are very red, and they make up about 50% of our blood by volume. RBCs are filled with hemoglobin that transports oxygen from our lungs throughout our bodies. RBCs are doughnut-shaped, but without a hole (see the red cell in the adjacent picture). Red blood cells, made in the bone marrow, do not have a nucleus or mitochondria, making them very pliable so they can squeeze through the smallest capillaries. They are like tiny balloons filled with hemoglobin and get their red color from the red hemoglobin that contains iron. Since they lack mitochondria, RBCs only use glycolysis to produce energy (ATP), but they do not need much

---

1. Landsteiner, "Ueber Agglutinationserscheinungen," 1132–34.

energy to transport oxygen, whereas muscle cells need lots of energy.

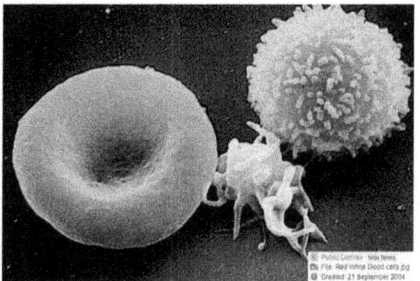

Red blood cell, activated platelet (yellow) & lymphocyte (blue) National Cancer Inst. Electron micrograph photo

Carbon Dioxide Transport

Carbon dioxide (CO_2) is a major waste product of our metabolism and since it is a gas we get rid of it by exhaling CO_2. The second role of RBCs is to convert carbon dioxide to bicarbonate, which requires the enzyme carbonic anhydrase. Without the conversion of CO_2 to carbonic acid that yields bicarbonate and a hydrogen ion (proton) our blood would be filled with bubbles of CO_2, much like soda pop. The proton helps hemoglobin release more oxygen in our tissues. Carbonic anhydrase, like all enzymes, catalyzes the reaction of CO_2 with water, and when RBCs reach the lungs, it catalyzes the conversion of bicarbonate back to water and CO_2 which is exhaled. Each molecule of glucose produces six molecules of CO_2, which is acidic. Bicarbonate is the primary buffer in our blood which prevents our blood from becoming acidic, and carbonic anhydrase allows our lungs to expel this acidic product of metabolism.

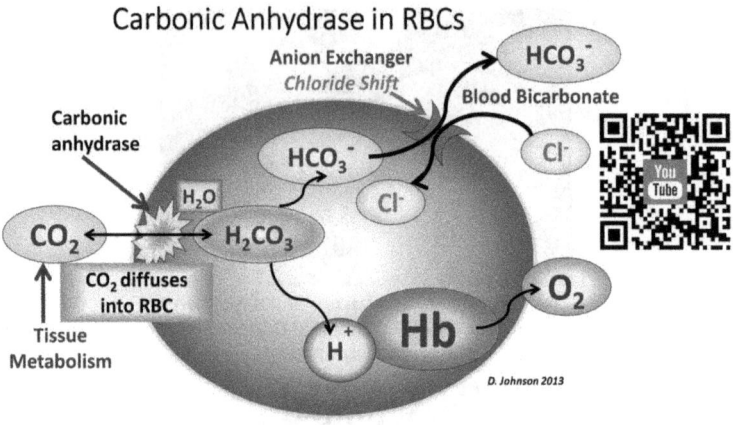

Heme Disposal and O_2 Saturation Measurement

When red blood cells die the heme group must be eliminated; thus it gets converted to compounds that make our poop brown and our urine yellow. Because oxygen is so important to life doctors and nurses use pulse oximeters to measure the percentage of our blood that is saturated with oxygen. Normal saturation levels are 95–100%, but patients with pneumonia, COVID-19, or emphysema will have abnormally low hemoglobin saturation. At 95% saturation, 95% of our hemoglobin molecules are carrying O_2, and only 5% of the hemoglobin molecules do not have bound O_2. Oxyhemoglobin absorbs more infrared light than red light, while deoxyhemoglobin absorbs more red light than infrared light. Pulse oximeters work by shining both types of red light on a fingertip and they measure the amounts of light passing through the blood vessel-rich tissue and calculate the percentage saturation. Smartwatches use a variation of this to measure reflected light.

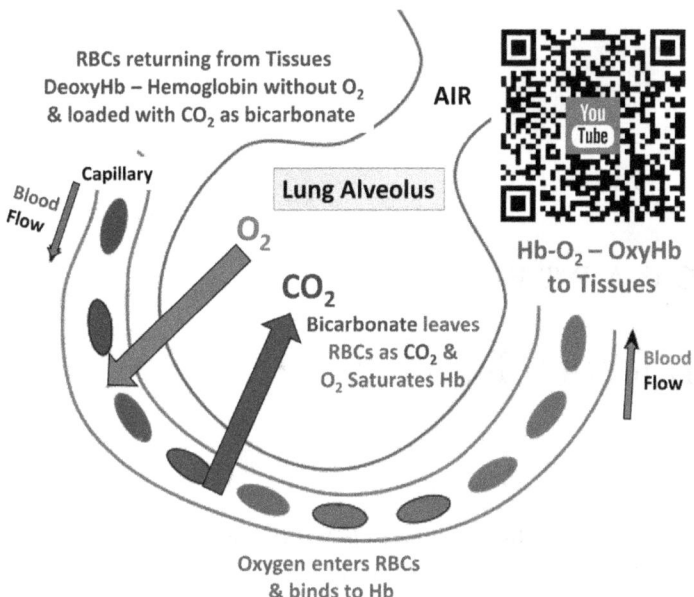

CHAPTER 12

Infection Fighters

"A plague o' both your houses!"
—WILLIAM SHAKESPEARE, ROMEO, AND JULIET (ACT 3, SCENE 1)[1], THE "PLAGUE" IS THE BUBONIC PLAGUE, WHICH RAVAGED EUROPE IN THE 14TH CENTURY.

Neutrophils Fight Infection

NEUTROPHILS MADE BY OUR bone marrow attack and kill invading bacteria and yeasts without the need for antibodies in a process called Innate Immunity. Additional members of the innate immunity task force include basophils, mast cells, and eosinophils. Neutrophils are the major "soldiers" in our battles against invading organisms because they can move from the blood into sites of infection. Neutrophils make our sputum green when we have a bacterial infection. So, when we have a cold or cough, doctors will often ask whether our sputum is clear suggesting a viral infection, or greenish indicating a bacterial infection, which can be treated with antibiotics. All our blood cells arise from a common stem cell as shown in the first figure in this chapter. Some people have abnormally low levels of neutrophils, a condition known as neutropenia that results in more frequent bacterial infections.

1. Shakespeare, *"Romeo and Juliet."*

Neutrophil levels are monitored by doctors because they increase in many bacterial infections, such as appendicitis. Deficiencies of vitamin B12 and folic acid, some cancers, and chemotherapy drugs can result in neutropenia, necessitating particular care to avoid infections.

Plasma Cells and Vaccinations

Plasma cells, also called B Lymphocytes (blue cells in the picture with red RBC), help fight infections by producing antibodies to foreign proteins, such as the coat proteins of bacteria and viruses. This process, which involves several cell types, is called Adaptive Immunity. Plasma cells make antibodies that protect us after we become infected by a pathogen or when we are immunized against various diseases. Depending on the pathogen or the quality of the vaccine it can take weeks to months to generate sufficient immunity to fight off the infection. Boosters increase the number of plasma cells making antibodies against a particular pathogen. After the infection has been beaten back, B lymphocytes, called memory cells persist for various lengths of time up to many years and they can quickly produce antibodies upon reinfection by the original pathogen. The slowness of the process for producing antibodies is why it takes a week or two to recover from colds or flu.

Smallpox made people extremely sick, with a mortality rate of about 30%, and left many of its victims with deep pitted facial scars and/or blindness. To protect his troops General George Washington had them intentionally infected in a process called variolation using a lancet to introduce smallpox scabs or pustule fluid into a scratch on the skin, resulting in only 0.5–3% mortality. Dr. Edward Jenner in rural England discovered that immunity could be produced by inoculating a person with material from a cowpox lesion that proved safer than variolation and avoided the risk of transmitting smallpox to others. Smallpox was eradicated in 1980 through a worldwide vaccination program. When I was a child, we all had scars on our shoulders where we had been vaccinated for smallpox; that we did not view as unsightly but as an assurance that we would not get smallpox.

CHAPTER 13

Blood Clotting

"How much more, then, will the blood of Christ, who through the eternal Spirit offered himself unblemished to God, cleanse our consciences from acts that lead to death, so that we may serve the living God!"
—(HEBREWS 9:14, NIV).

Platelets Plug Cuts

HAVE YOU EVER WONDERED how a cut finger stops bleeding? Platelets (yellow in the picture with red RBC) are small, fragments of megakaryocytes. When we cut our fingers or have blood vessel damage, platelets are the first responders and stick to exposed collagen fibers of the vessel wall. Platelets stick to each other and to fibrinogen at the site of injury, followed by the conversion of fibrinogen to insoluble fibrin that strengthens the clot and stops bleeding so the injury can heal. Aspirin reduces platelet function or stickiness, and doctors often prescribe aspirin to slow blood clotting in patients who have had a heart attack or who have coronary artery stents. Platelets are renewed about every 10 days, so patients are often told to stop aspirin therapy a week before elective surgery.

Blood Clotting

Blood clotting is a vital process that keeps us from bleeding to death when we cut our fingers or have an injury, and it is important that the bleeding stops in a reasonable length of time. Those who bleed too much are said to have hemophilia. Clotting involves several irreversible enzymatic changes to blood proteins ending with the conversion of soluble fibrinogen to insoluble fibrin. While platelets initially plug the cut like a finger in a dyke, fibrin ties the platelets together in a mesh that stabilizes the clot to prevent further bleeding. Fibrin-rich scabs protect the tissue until healing occurs. The enzyme that converts fibrinogen to fibrin is thrombin, (thrombosis is another word for a blood clot). Thrombin, like pancreatic trypsin, is a protease that breaks peptide bonds in proteins, but thrombin specifically cleaves fibrinogen into fibrin. Patients who have had a heart attack or who have had surgery are often treated with drugs that slow down blood clotting. Warfarin has been used since the 1950s to slow clotting because it reduces the amount of thrombin by inhibiting a vitamin K (German spelling of coagulation - Koagulation) a required step in making thrombin.

Rat Poison Discovery

Mysteriously dairy cows in Wisconsin were bleeding to death, causing a major economic loss. A farmer went to the University of Wisconsin College of Agriculture with a dead cow, and the moldy sweet clover the cow had been fed. The UW veterinary faculty discovered that coumarin, a chemical in spoiled sweet clover, was the culprit. In 1940 they synthesized dicumarol that slowed blood clotting and named it WARFarin because the Wisconsin Alumni Research Foundation (WARF) had supported their research efforts. Warfarin was also used to poison mice and rats since they would bleed to death if they ate too much, but because some rats have become resistant its use for this has declined. Patients on Warfarin must be carefully monitored via blood samples regarding how well their blood is clotting because too much Warfarin causes bleeding. Diet is also important because some foods have more vitamin K than others. For example, spinach is rich in vitamin K, and using an oily salad dressing results in more vitamin K being absorbed by the body, because vitamin K is a fat-soluble vitamin.

Hemophilia and the Russian Revolution

Some defects in our genes are caused by mutations. Each of us has twenty-three pairs of chromosomes of which the 23rd is different in men and women and known as the sex chromosome. In men, this chromosome is described as XY while in women it is XX. Queen Victoria became known as the "grandmother of Europe" through the marriages of her children to other royal families in Europe. Victoria was the great-grandmother of Alexei Romanov, the son of Tsar Nicholas II and Tsarina Alexandra of Russia and heir to the throne. X-linked genetic diseases are carried by women who do not have the disease because their other good X chromosome is sufficient to prevent disease manifestation. Such X-linked diseases are often seen in the sons of carriers who have inherited the bad X genome rather than the good one. Alexi had inherited X-linked Type B hemophilia from Victoria in which blood clotting factor nine is defective, preventing the activation of thrombin, and consequently, fibrinogen is not converted to insoluble fibrin needed for stable blood clots. The mystic Rasputin won favor with the Royal family when he recommended stopping Alexi's treatment with aspirin, one of the first commercial drugs now known to increase bleeding: aspirin was only making his condition worse. Type B hemophilia causes bruising and bleeding due to the inability to make functional thrombin.

Research on blood clotting enzymes has resulted in several new drugs for preventing the formation of life-threatening blood clots that occur in heart attacks and strokes. Excess bleeding can also be life-threatening, especially in injuries on the battlefield or accidents, and drugs to stop bleeding have been developed through blood clotting research. Hemophilia A results from a genetic deficiency of blood clotting factor eight and factor eight protein isolated from pooled units of human blood was used for years to treat it. Unfortunately, several children became infected with HIV from contaminated blood before it was realized that HIV was a contaminant. Recombinant factor eight is now available for treating hemophilia A, which avoids the risk of using blood from human donors that could contain some new unknown disease agent.

Endothelium the Blood Vessel Lining

Blood pressure results from our hearts pumping blood throughout our bodies. Endothelium, the tissue lining the inside of the vessels, is like a bicycle tire inner tube for our blood vessels. Collagen and other structural proteins strengthen the blood vessel walls while smooth muscle cells control the diameter of blood vessels to help regulate blood pressure. Our approximately 60,000 miles of blood vessels have a one-cell thick lining of endothelial cells. Endothelium is in constant contact with our blood, where it plays a fundamental role in maintaining cardiovascular health by regulating blood flow, preventing thrombosis, controlling inflammation, facilitating nutrient exchange, and promoting repair. Endothelium cells are intimately involved in preventing blood clots when they are not needed and in aiding the clotting process when blood vessels are damaged. People with coronary artery disease often have chest pains called angina due to the narrowing of arteries and reduced blood flow, which is relieved by nitroglycerin tablets.

Nitroglycerin and Angina

Alfred Nobel, who founded the Nobel Prizes, discovered dynamite which is nitroglycerin mixed with diatomaceous earth (diatomite). Nitroglycerin was difficult to work with because it would explode if shaken, whereas dynamite was very stable until ignited with a black powder blasting cap. After workers in the dynamite factory reported less angina pain on workdays, a physician in London started using nitroglycerin in 1876 to treat angina. However, it was not until 1977 that researchers discovered that nitroglycerin was being metabolized to nitric oxide, which had long been called endothelial relaxing factor. Enzymes in endothelial cells convert the amino acid arginine to nitric oxide (NO), a colorless gas that relaxes the smooth muscles surrounding blood vessels, improving blood flow. Arginine, an amino acid, is used by our endothelial cells to make nitric oxide, which helps lower blood pressure. Nitroglycerin is still being used to treat angina. While Pfizer was testing the drug sildenafil as a potential alternative treatment for angina based on increasing NO blood levels, a side effect reported by male volunteers led to its use as a treatment for impotence and pulmonary arterial hypertension[1], but patients taking this drug are cautioned not to also take nitroglycerin or other nitrates.

---

1. Ghofrani et al., "Sildenafil."

CHAPTER 14

Hydrogen Bonds in DNA

"We have caught the first glimpse of our own instruction book, previously known only to God."
- FRANCIS COLLINS, M.D. PH.D. DIRECTOR OF THE NIH IN THE EAST ROOM OF THE WHITE HOUSE JUNE, 6 2000 WHEN PRESIDENT CLINTON ANNOUNCED THE FIRST DRAFT OF THE HUMAN GENOME SEQUENCE.[1]

PCR Revolutionized the Study of DNA

HOW IS IT POSSIBLE to get DNA from fingerprints? This may seem like magic, but it is a molecular biology technique called PCR (Polymerase Chain Reaction) used in many labs. PCR takes advantage of the weak H-bonds holding DNA strands together. Thermophilic bacteria can grow at elevated temperatures 65–70 °C (149–158 °F) that would kill other organisms. *Thermus aquaticus* was isolated from hot springs in Yellowstone National Park, and its Taq DNA polymerase enzyme made the PCR possible. PCR allows forensic scientists to amplify the tiny amounts of DNA in a fingerprint. In the first step of PCR, the two strands of the DNA double helix are separated by heating, a process called nucleic acid denaturation, which breaks the H-bonds between the strands. When

1. Khullar, "Faith, Science."

the temperature is lowered, short sequences of single-stranded DNA (called primers) bind to the complementary sequences of DNA. The two DNA strands then become templates for Taq DNA polymerase to enzymatically assemble a new DNA strand using a mixture of A, T, G, and C deoxynucleotide triphosphates, (DNA building blocks). As PCR progresses, the new DNA is also used as a template for replication, setting in motion a chain reaction in which the original DNA template is exponentially amplified via repeated heating and cooling steps of a device called a thermocycler that holds microliter test tubes. DNA of thermophilic bacteria have a higher GC content than bacteria that live at room temperature called mesophiles. The GC-rich sequences of thermophiles code for amino acids that also make their enzymes, such as Taq DNA polymerase, stable at elevated temperatures. PCR allows forensic scientists to amplify the DNA sequences found in the fingerprints at crime scenes to billions of copies that can be sequenced. PCR tests were also the "gold standard" for COVID-19 testing.

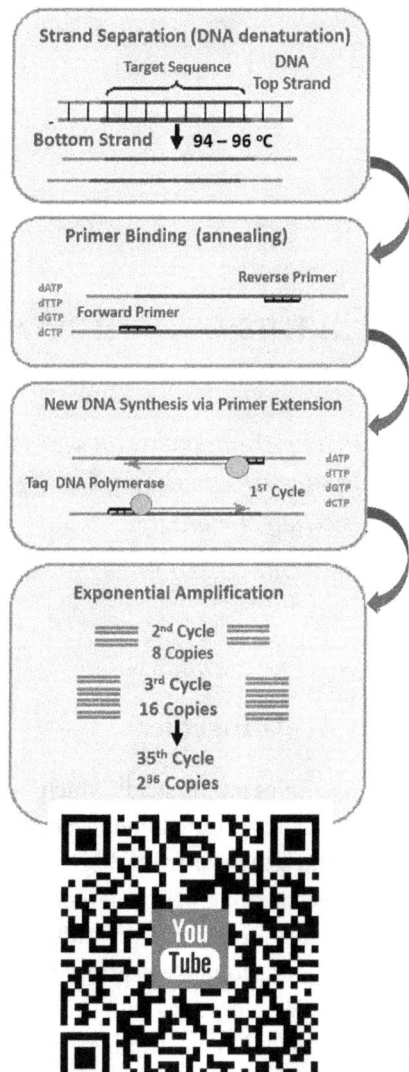

CHAPTER 15

Proteins: Chains of Amino Acids

"Science is the search for truth, that is the effort to understand the world: it involves the rejection of bias, of dogma, of revelation, but not the rejection of morality."
—LINUS PAULING, NOBEL LAUREATE[1]

Linking Amino Acids Together

PROTEINS ARE MADE UP of amino acids which can be viewed as molecules of ammonia and acetic acid (vinegar) linked through an alpha carbon from which their different R-groups extend. It is the R-group that makes each amino acid different because the rest of the molecule is the same for each. Amino acids are linked together in chains via peptide bonds to make peptides consisting of two or more amino acids into large proteins with thousands of amino acids. The sequence in which they are arranged from the N-terminus to the carboxyl terminus is called primary structure, like pearls on a string as seen in an earlier figure.

1. Pauling, "Science is search."

Proteins: Chains of Amino Acids

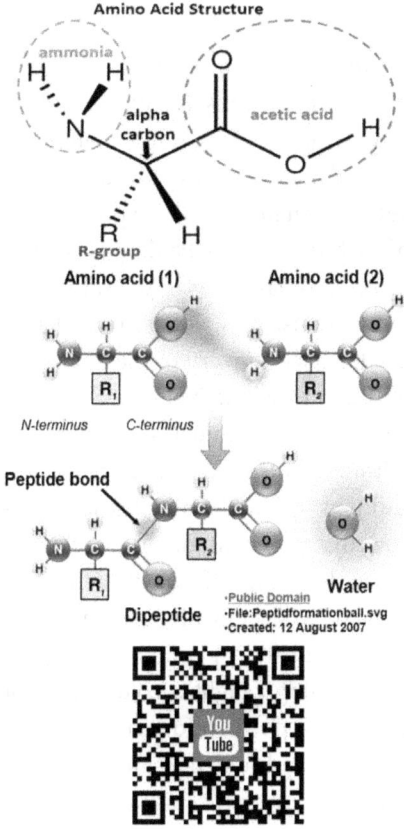

The importance of H-bonds in holding DNA strands together has already been discussed. Hydrogen bonds are also important in the structure of proteins. The sequence of amino acids in a protein is called the Primary structure and the next level is the Secondary structure. The 3D folding of a protein is its Tertiary structure and proteins with more than one polypeptide chain, such as hemoglobin have a Quaternary structure (how the pieces fit together). The structures of the twenty amino acids are pictured in Chapter 16, for those who might be interested.

Alpha Helix

Wool and silk are proteins for clothing, but what makes wool warm and stretchy, whereas silk is smooth and strong? Two secondary structures discovered by Linus Pauling are stabilized by hydrogen bonds and are known as the alpha helix and beta sheet. These structures are seen in virtually all proteins with some having more or less of each type. Linus Pauling is considered one of the top twenty scientists to have ever lived and he is the only person to have received two unshared Nobel Prizes. Pauling received his first Nobel prize for his discovery of the alpha helix in chemistry (1954), and his second was the Nobel Peace Prize (1962), for his activism for peace and against nuclear weapons. In 1951 Pauling's passport was withheld by the US State Department to prevent him from participating in international conferences. Pauling was also the first to show that a genetic disease (sickle cell anemia) had a molecular cause due to a different protein structure. Pauling's work on the alpha helix began with determining the crystal structure of amino acids and short peptides. During a visit to Oxford, England in 1948 Pauling caught a cold. He spent some time in bed resting and drew a polypeptide chain of roughly the correct dimensions on paper and folded it into a helix, carefully maintaining the planar peptide bonds, resulting in a model with physically plausible hydrogen bonds for his first Nobel Prize.[2] The alpha helix has 3.6 amino acid residues per turn, and it is stabilized by hydrogen bonds between the amide hydrogen of one amino acid and carbonyl oxygen four amino acids away. All amino acids have the same structure but differ concerning their R-groups which stick out from the cylindrical helix core, allowing interaction of these functional groups with other protein R-groups. Two alpha helixes are shown in the picture below. The red ribbon in the one on the left is superimposed on the peptide chain to show the helix more clearly. The image on the right shows the green hydrogen bonds that stabilize the alpha helix. An alpha helix-rich protein is wool which contributes to its stretchiness and warmth. Human hair is keratin which consists of multiple alpha helical coiled coils.

2. Pauling, L. et al. "Structure of Proteins," 205–11.

Keratins also make up fingernails and toenails, and fifty-four genes are coding for different keratins. Eastern Bluebirds do not have blue pigment in their feathers, but they appear blue because keratin in their feathers refracts blue light.

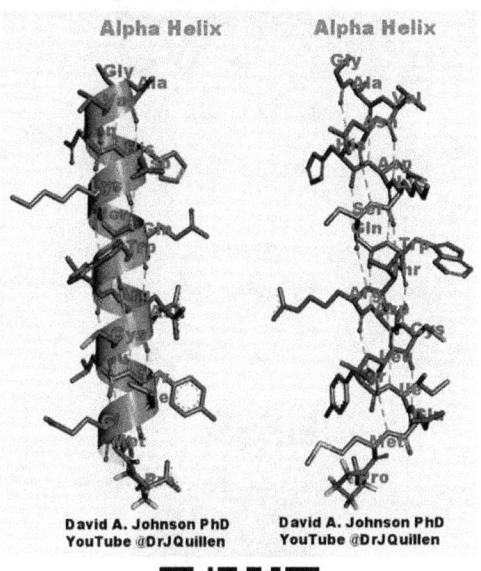

Alpha Helix
Red Ribbon and H-bonds

David A. Johnson PhD
YouTube @DrJQuillen

Beta Sheet

Beta sheet secondary structure is stabilized by H-bonds between two protein chains organized in a linear, side-by-side fashion held together by hydrogen bonds between amino hydrogen and carbonyl oxygen, resulting in a rather flat structure, also discovered by Pauling. The H-bonding can be between two parallel protein sequences or between anti-parallel sequences. Silk is a beta sheet-rich protein with a high glycine content resulting in hydrogen R-groups above and below the sheet, making silk smooth and strong.

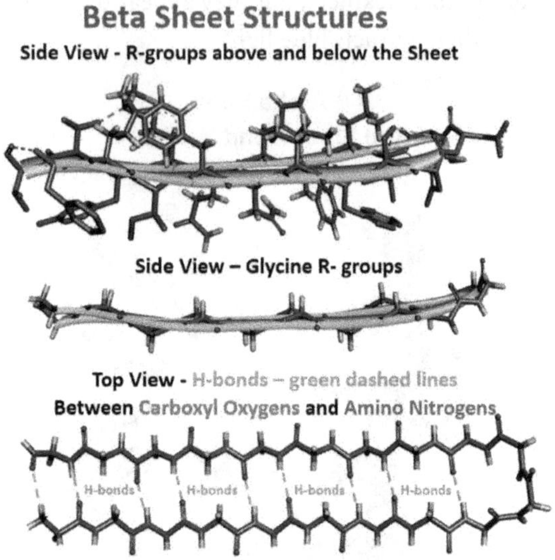
Beta Sheet Structures
Side View - R-groups above and below the Sheet
Side View – Glycine R- groups
Top View - H-bonds – green dashed lines
Between Carboxyl Oxygens and Amino Nitrogens
H-bonds
H-bonds
H-bonds
H-bonds

Amino Acid Structures – The Words of Life

The structures of the amino acids are shown below for reference for those who might be interested. Each amino acid has different chemical properties based on structure. The essential amino acids are noted with a green *. Note that the red colored portions of each amino acid are the same and these are involved in linking the amino acids together. When they are linked into proteins the negative and positive charges are lost because they form the peptide bonds in the protein strand. The blue portions are each different and they are important to 3D folding and the function of the protein, such as its enzymatic activity.

Disulfide Bonds

Another important bond in proteins is the disulfide bond that can form between two cysteine sulfurs in proteins. Insulin has two disulfide bonds holding its two protein chains together. Disulfide bonds are also involved in other protein structures. For example, people with straight hair sometimes get permanent curls or waves in their hair, and some who have curly hair get it straightened. Hair is a protein called keratin and it is rich in its content of cysteine amino acids. Disulfide bonds can be broken by treating the hair with solutions of cysteine or other compounds with sulfhydryl groups, followed by straightening or curling, then air oxidation allows disulfide bonds to form while the hair is curled or straight that will then keep the hair curly or straight. Two cysteines linked by a disulfide bond are referred to as cystine.

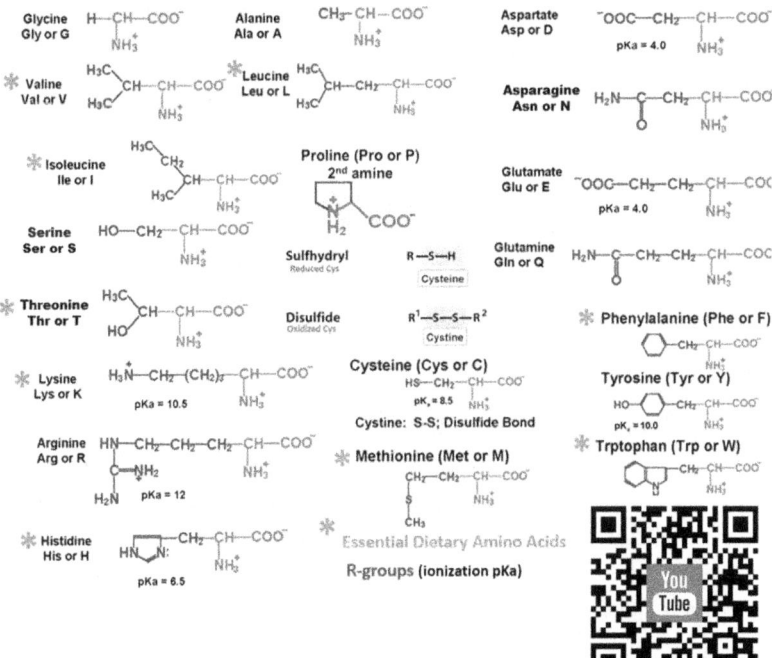

CHAPTER 16

Proteins and Diet

"Let food be thy medicine and medicine be thy food."
—HIPPOCRATES, GREEK PHYSICIAN (C. 460-370 BC)[1].

"The only way to keep your health is to eat what you don't want, drink what you don't like, and do what you'd rather not."
—MARK TWAIN, AMERICAN AUTHOR (1835-1910).[2]

Nine Amino Acids Are Essential for Humans

HUMANS LACK THE METABOLIC machinery to make nine of the twenty amino acids that we must have to live. These nine nutritionally essential amino acids can only be obtained through our diet. They are **Histidine, Methionine, Threonine, Valine, Isoleucine, Phenylalanine, Tryptophan, Leucine, and Lysine.** All the other eleven can be synthesized from the carbohydrates in our diets. If our diets lack any one of the essential amino acids, we will not be able to make the proteins that need that amino acid, which can result in stunted growth, muscle wasting, disease, and

1. Hippocrates, *"Let food be thy medicine."*
2. Twain, *"Only Way to Keep."*

even death. Nutrition is important, and all dietary proteins are not created equal. Dietary proteins must not only have all the essential amino acids, but they must also be easily digested to provide our needed nutrition. The best measure of protein quality for human nutrition is the Digestible Indispensable Amino Acid Score (DIAAS), which is calculated based on the amounts of essential amino acids absorbed by the body and the amount of that amino acid required for human growth and development. High-quality proteins have DIAAS values of 100% or higher. Animal proteins tend to have higher DIAAS values than plant proteins, so vegans need to eat more and varied plant sources to get adequate amounts of the essential amino acids. Additionally, only meats, fish, poultry, dairy, and eggs contain vitamin B12, the absence of which can result in severe anemia and death. Fortunately, vegans can take B12 supplements, and many plant-based foods have B12 added during processing. Still, hundreds of millions of people in the world lack adequate protein nutrition which can have life-long negative health effects.

Milk

The most important protein for humans and other mammals is milk casein because it contains the ideal mixture of essential amino acids to nurture babies and other mammal infants. Casein, the most abundant milk protein, lacks the 3D structure seen in hemoglobin and trypsin because its purpose is to be digested. Casein's unfolded structure allows our digestive enzymes to easily break it up into individual amino acids that can then enter our blood and nourish our organs. Proteins that we refer to as "denatured" lack their normal 3D structure. Cooking denatures proteins and makes them more easily digestible, as well as killing microorganisms. Mother's milk is our best nutritional source of protein; easy to digest and just what babies need. Milk also contains lactose which is a disaccharide (sugar) of galactose and glucose, and virtually all infants have intestinal lactase that allows them to digest lactose so they can metabolize the sugars. Most mammals and many humans become lactose intolerant after they are weaned from their mother's milk. The majority of people of northern European descent and other populations that domesticated dairy animals (cows and goats) retain the ability to metabolize lactose due to a long history of their ancestors drinking milk and eating dairy. People who are lactose intolerant or allergic to milk often substitute plant-based "milk" (soy milk, almond milk, coconut, or oat milk) which is fortified with calcium and vitamins. Still, these lack the high-quality protein content of human or cow milk. The table below lists the relative amounts of lactose, carbohydrates, protein, fats, and calories, along with the DIAAS of each protein source. Human milk is by far our best source of protein nutrition. Of the plant-based sources only soy comes close to the protein quality of human milk. Almond, coconut, and oat milk formulations are extremely low in protein and essential amino acids. FairLife® milk is cow milk that has been filtered to remove most of the lactose and treated with lactase to digest what remains, and the process increases protein and calcium content. We use FairLife in our home, which has a long shelf-life because it is ultra-pasteurized. Infants need high-fat milk for brain development because it contains fatty acids needed for the formation of myelin, the fatty sheath that insulates nerve cells and aids cognition. Mother's milk contains more fat than protein, emphasizing the importance of fats in human infant nutrition. Many pediatricians recommend that infants be breastfed from birth until at least one year old, and then supplement other foods with whole milk until they are two years old to aid brain development. Mother's milk also contains antibodies that protect infants from infections and no other protein sources or infant formulas provide the antibodies in mother's milk. The amounts of protein, fat, and lactose in a mother's milk vary over time and change to meet the baby's nutritional needs. The quality of the mother's milk also depends on her diet.

Table 1

Milks Approximate Content per cup (240ml)						
Milk	Lactose	Carbs	Protein	Fats	Calories	DIAAS
Human	17g	17g	3g	8.6g	168	122%
Cow (whole)	17g	12g	8g	9.4g	149	118%
Cow (1%)	12g	12g	8g	2.3g	102	118%
Soy (plain)	0g	12g	7g	4.0g	80	90%
Almond (plain)	0g	0g	1g	3.0g	35	40%
Coconut (plain)	0g	0g	0g	3.5g	35	36%
Oat (plain)	2g	0g	1g	0g	60	50%
FairLife (cow whole)	0g	6g	1g	5.0g	150	118%

Human Milk Composition https://www.ncbi.nlm.nih.gov/pmc/articles/PMC3586783/

Plant Milk Compositions https://www.hsph.harvard.edu/nutritionsource/milk/

Google Bard AI "What are the DIAAS of human milk, cow milk, soy milk, almond milk, coconut milk, and oat milk?" Accessed July 11, 2023

DIAAS% are based on absorption of essential amino acids and the amount of that amino acid required for human growth and development.

Eggs

Eggs are another very good source of high-quality protein with a DIAAS of 100%. Interestingly, "Eiweiss" is Germain for protein, and egg white is the goopy stuff that surrounds the egg yolk. It is a high-quality protein (rich in essential amino acids, needed in our diet). Cooked eggs are the next best substitute for cow milk for essential amino acids. When eggs are cooked the clear protein liquid (albumin) becomes white and solid because it has been denatured. The function of egg white is to provide the baby birds with the amino acids they need to grow into chicks. Whipping egg white denatures the protein and the air mixed in causes the protein to surround the tiny air bubbles. With continued beating using an electric mixer or whisk more air will be added increasing the volume about eight times that of the original egg whites, resulting in a white fluffy semisolid meringue. Adding sugar and/or cream of tartar (potassium bitartrate) makes the foam stronger. Soft meringue is often used to top pies that are then lightly browned in an oven. Baking meringue at a low temperature (250 degrees F), followed by letting it sit in a warm oven overnight dries out the water and makes the meringue firm and crunchy.

CHAPTER 17

Creation and Science

"Science investigates religion interprets. Science gives man knowledge which is power religion gives man wisdom which is control."

—MARTIN LUTHER KING, JR.[1]

Creation of Humans with Souls

NUMEROUS CREATION STORIES FROM various cultures and religions have been reported around the world. Genesis, the first book of the Jewish Torah, contains two creation stories. In Genesis 1 man and woman are created on the sixth day. *"So God created mankind in his own image, in the image of God he created them; male and female he created them."* (Genesis 1:27, NIV) In Genesis 2, man is made from dust, and the breath of life, a living soul, is breathed into him. *"Then the Lord God formed a man from the dust of the ground and breathed into his nostrils the breath of life, and the man became a living being."* (Genesis 2:7, NIV) The King James and some other versions have *"and man became a living soul."* The gospel of John tells us that Jesus Christ was with God at the time of creation. Genesis 1 states that God created man, the heavens,

---

1. King, Science investigates.

the earth, and all life in six days. However, 2 Peter 3:8 states, *"But, beloved, be not ignorant of this one thing, that one day is with the Lord as a thousand years and a thousand years as one day."*(NIV) So, times recorded in ancient texts may be far from accurate. The Islamic Qur'an also has a six-day creation story, and both the Jewish and the Muslim monotheistic religions regard Abraham as a father figure. The theory of relativity predicts what is called "time dilation" in that time passes more slowly for objects moving at high speeds or in strong gravitational fields. While it is physically impossible for us to travel at the speed of light, after a trip of five years to and from another galaxy at 99% the speed of light people on Earth would have aged 35.5 years.[2] This was the basic idea behind the movie *"Back to the Future"*, starring Michael J. Fox as Marty McFly. God would not be constrained by physics, so God's time scale is beyond our ability to comprehend. Creation appears to be complete by the end of Genesis 1, but Genesis 2 is more descriptive of the creation of man and woman, with a living soul being bestowed via the breath of life. The time between Chapter 1 and Chapter 2 is not stated, so it could be a short time or thousands of years. Many people who have had their DNA analyzed found out that they have genes inherited from Neanderthals who lived between about 130,000 and 40,000 years ago. Some modern humans also have DNA from Denisovans (500,000 to 30,000 years ago) and Homo erectus (two million to 117,000 years ago). The fossil record indicates that anatomically modern humans, Homo sapiens, occurred in Africa around 300,000 to 200,000 years ago. Thus, in agreement with the two creation stories in Genesis, the logical conclusion is that humanoids existed on Earth for hundreds of thousands of years before God "breathed life into them" giving humans souls.

---

2. Einstein, "Elektrodynamik Bewegter" 891–921.

C.S. Lewis on the creation of man with a soul

> "For long centuries God perfected the animal form which was to become the vehicle of humanity and the image of Himself. He gave it hands whose thumb could be applied to each of the fingers, and jaws and teeth and throat capable of articulation, and a brain sufficiently complex to execute all the material motions whereby rational thought is incarnated. The creature may have existed for ages in this state before it became man: it may even have been clever enough to make things that a modern archaeologist would accept as proof of its humanity. But it was only an animal because all its physical and psychical processes were directed to purely material and natural ends. Then, in the fullness of time, God caused to descend upon this organism, both on its psychology and physiology, a new kind of consciousness that could say "I" and "me," which could look upon itself as an object, which knew God, which could make judgments of truth, beauty, and goodness, and which was so far above time that it could perceive time flowing past".[3] This quote is consistent with the conclusion that the Earth is billions of years old, and man (in various forms) existed for hundreds of thousands of years before being made human by receiving a soul.

"Every good and perfect gift is from above, coming down from the Father of the heavenly lights, who does not change like shifting shadows." (James 1:17, NIV). And "For my thoughts are not your thoughts, neither are your ways my ways," declares the LORD. "As the heavens are higher than the earth, so are my ways higher than your ways and my thoughts than your thoughts." (Isaiah 55:8–9, NIV).

Some people believe that the earth and all life were made about 10,000 years ago based on a literal interpretation of Genesis. They reject scientific dating methods, such as radiometric dating and geological evidence, which estimate the age of the Earth at 4.5 billion years. A young Earth belief necessitates that God created

---

3. Lewis, "Problem of pain," 67–8.

fossils, old radiological specimens, and old skeletal remains, such as dinosaur and Neanderthal bones when the Earth was formed. It is impossible to scientifically disprove this view which is based on faith and not science. Bible stories of the Garden of Eden and Noah's Ark teach some wonderful lessons about God and faith, and I, like many Christian children who were taught these stories, loved them. However, we now know there are over 6,000 recognized species of mammals, which were far too many for Noah to have carried on the Ark. Regardless of one's beliefs, the molecules of life (DNA and amino acids) are the same in all living things on Earth.

"Love never fails. But where there are prophecies, they will cease; where there are tongues, they will be stilled; where there is knowledge, it will pass away. For we know in part, and we prophesy in part, but when completeness comes, what is in part disappears. When I was a child, I talked like a child, I thought like a child, I reasoned like a child. When I became a man, I put the ways of childhood behind me. For now, we see only a reflection as in a mirror; then we shall see face to face. Now I know in part; then I shall know fully, even as I am fully known." (1 Corinthians 13:8–12, NIV).

Genesis Creation Stories

The first creation story is in Genesis 1 and there is a second account in Genesis 2. Although the creation of the universe, as well as man and woman, are stated in Genesis there are no scientific details, such as the genetic makeup of living things. Genesis is more about God and man's relationship to God than about science. Most religions credit a great power for creating the universe and life because there is no way to know how the universe came into existence. Even the most powerful telescopes which are finding new stars, new planets, and black holes do not provide clues about their creation.

Albert Einstein said in referring to himself as a scientist, "His religious feeling takes the form of a rapturous amazement at the harmony of natural law, which reveals an intelligence of such

CREATION AND SCIENCE

superiority that, compared with it, all the systematic thinking and acting of human beings is an utterly insignificant reflection."[4] (*The World as I See It* essay 1930). According to the Big Bang theory, the universe began as a hot, dense point, known as a singularity, about 13.8 billion years ago. Scientific evidence supporting the Big Bang theory includes the cosmic microwave background radiation, which is believed to be the leftover radiation from the Big Bang, and the observed redshift of distant galaxies, which suggests that the universe is expanding. It is worth noting that the Big Bang theory does not explain its origin, only what happened after the Big Bang. The scientific evidence for the Big Bang is a theory that science will evaluate and refine. Who or what caused the Big Bang remains a mystery. God is also mysterious in that no one has ever seen God, except Moses who witnessed Him in a burning bush (Exodus 3) and saw His back (Exodus 33). Many people pray to God as a father figure, but a being capable of creating the universe is beyond the ability of humans to comprehend. Humans long to understand the mind of God because we know our lives are finite and we do not understand what happens when life ends. Christians believe in the Trinity of God (the Father), Jesus Christ (the Son), and the Holy Spirit (the Comforter) and life everlasting through belief in Jesus Christ as the Son of God. Yet we ponder what that life will be like because we know that our physical bodies will decay and turn to dust. Our pride causes us to think that we can understand the mind of God and what the future holds. But alas, as St. Augustine told us in the fourth century *"It was pride that changed angels into devils; it is humility that makes men as angels."*[5]

The Torah (which was Jewish scripture before Christians adopted it) and other ancient religious writings focus on a creator or spirit that many believe exists, but a spirit beyond our comprehension. Faith is mystical, whereas science is hard facts. Science is based on testable hypotheses, whereas theology is about faith in the unseen. Creation beliefs are based on faith and have no scientific basis. False teachers argue that creationism is science, but it

---

4. Einstein, "World as I See It."
5. Augustine, "pride that changed."

is fake science. Many people view creation as an evolving process of creative activity, with the laws of chemistry and physics serving as the mechanisms through which God operates. Science and our understanding of evolution provide evidence that the Earth and the solar system are constantly changing, but it tells us nothing about who or why it all began.

Evolution is Not Scary

Evolution seems to be a scary word for many people, but evolution is a scientifically accepted theory well-documented. Theory is not just someone's thoughts or an idea, but a well-substantiated explanation of some aspect of the natural world, based on repeated observations and experiments. Evolution is one of the most well-supported theories in science, and it explains how populations of organisms change over time, resulting from the accumulation of genetic mutations. Evolution does not oppose God, but rather it explains how God achieves his purposes. Evolution is not a purposeless process, nor does it replace God or substitute for God in any way. Mutations can be beneficial and aid an organism in survival and better reproduction, thus passing on the advantage to offspring. Mutations can be harmful and cause disease or reduce survival or reproduction. Finally, mutations can be neutral, providing no advantages or disadvantages. Without evolution, farmers could not breed better livestock, such as cows that produce more milk. For eons farmers saved their best grains and seeds to plant the following year, slowly evolving better crops. Scientists have modified plant genes to make them resistant to herbicides, so weeds do not consume the fertilizer needed for crops. If God had not incorporated the ability to evolve, why have things changed over time? God gave his living creations the ability to change and adapt over time, so they could survive and improve. Individuals also change over time in that we learn new skills and abilities, and hopefully we become more kind and more loving of others. In studying proteins, I have seen evolution many times in the amino acid sequences of proteins. Fortunately, we are all different, which makes for an interesting world. What a dull existence we would have if all men looked like Adam and all women looked like Eve.

Genetic Diversity Makes Life Beautiful

Genetic diversity results in differences in protein amino acid sequences, for example, many hemoglobin molecules have slightly different amino acid sequences making them better or poorer transporters of oxygen, relative to the norm. Humans make different hemoglobins at distinct stages of development. Embryos have Zeta and Epsilon hemoglobins during the first three months of gestation corresponding to the alpha and beta subunits of adult hemoglobin, respectively. Zeta-Hb is replaced by the Alpha subunit, whereas Epsilon is replaced by the Gamma subunit, which aids the transfer of oxygen from the mother's hemoglobin to the fetus. Hemoglobin with Alpha and Gamma subunits is called fetal hemoglobin. During the last three months of gestation, the Beta subunit begins to replace the Gamma subunit and this process is usually complete 6 months after we are born. Humans also make a small amount of Delta subunits, which are Beta-like but slightly different. Newborns have 10–30% Delta subunits, whereas adults have only 2–3.5%. Although the Delta subunit functions like the Beta subunit, why adults still have a small amount is a mystery.

The sequence homologies of several proteins support the theory of evolution. All vertebrates have red blood cells with hemoglobin, and the various hemoglobin proteins are remarkably similar in sequence and structure. Hemoglobin molecules of varied species can provide advantages or disadvantages. For example, crocodile hemoglobin helps them stay submerged for extended periods and helps them kill their prey, such as the water buffalo. Crocodile hemoglobin is different from mammalian hemoglobin in that it has a binding site for bicarbonate, resulting from food oxidative metabolism. When crocodiles grab their prey, they pull it underwater to drown it. Crocodile hemoglobin releases more oxygen to their muscles as blood bicarbonate increases during the struggle. Their more oxygen-efficient hemoglobin allows them to win the struggle for life, and then they dine at their leisure.

Cytochrome C is another protein that uses heme groups to oxidize our fuels to CO_2 and water. Cytochrome Cs are found in all eukaryotes (all plants, animals, fungi, and many algae) and the different eukaryotic cytochrome C proteins are very similar in sequence and structure to human cytochrome C. Insulin, a small protein hormone needed for cells to take in glucose, is found in all vertebrates, from fish to humans, and they too are very similar in sequence and structure. The similarity of animal insulins allowed type 1 diabetes to be treated for many years using insulin purified from the pancreas of cows and pigs. Those insulins that saved the lives of many children with Type 1 (juvenile) diabetes differed from human insulin by just a few amino acids. Unfortunately, some patients developed immunity to them because their bodies saw their slight differences as "foreign" proteins like invading bacteria or viruses and attacked them. Now recombinant human insulin is being produced by engineered microorganisms. Pharmaceutical companies used this technology to make a few changes in their amino acid sequences to produce short-acting and long-acting insulins, as well as other useful forms. Virus proteins mutate and evolve much faster than animals, enabling them to infect us more easily or to make us sick. God gave man a soul, just as God gives the Holy Spirit, but no experiment can be performed to assess the presence of either. Yet, spiritual changes can be seen in people who focus on loving God and loving others.

The Bible is Not a Science Book

The Bible is not a science book, but a book of faith that tells of man's relationship with God and with fellow humans. There are examples of love and cruel brutality, as well as the value of prayer and faith. The Psalms and Proverbs are poetic and wisdom literature that enlighten us regarding the relationship of man to God. *"But you, Lord, are a compassionate and gracious God, slow to anger, abounding in love and faithfulness."* (Psalm 86:15, NIV). Bibles are chronologically ordered with the Old Testament before the New Testament. but as a Christian, I feel that the Good News of Jesus is more important and that the New Testament should come before Jewish history.

"Creation Science" began in 1946 with a book by Henry Morris, an engineer, who wrote "*That You Might Believe*"[6], to answer some claims of evolution. This was before scientists had worked out the structure of DNA and amino acids or proteins. "Creation Science" is not science, rather it is faith or belief in the creation story as presented in Genesis. "Creation Science" has also become a multimillion-dollar business. Creation science is a pseudoscience that attempts to use the Bible to disprove scientific theories. Most creation scientists do not research disease to improve health, but rather spend their time giving paid lectures and writing books to make money from people's faith. Creation scientists often use cherry-picked data and faulty reasoning to support claims that are detrimental to both science and faith. For example, Creationists often cherry-pick radiometric errors with inaccurate ages for rocks and fossils, while ignoring the overwhelming consensus among geologists and scientists that radiometric dating methods are dependable and provide accurate ages. Creationists claim irreducible complexity of biological structures, such as the eye, but science has shown that the eye could have evolved gradually from simple light-sensitive cells.[7] Many eye proteins, such as opsin and crystallin, are found in all animals with sight, from jellyfish to humans and there is evidence for their molecular evolution. Creationists also claim that the Cambrian Explosion (five-hundred million years ago) during which the fossil record documents an increase in animal diversity favor creation rather than evolution via natural selection. But the Cambrian Explosion may not have been as dramatic as it seems, due to the incompleteness of the fossil record, because soft-bodied animals do not leave fossils. Also, there is the possibility that fossils of earlier species have just not been found. Finally, genetic molecular data have revealed new phylogenetic relationships

6. Morris, "That You Might Believe."
7. Glaeser, "*Evolution of the Eye*".

and filled gaps in the fossil record.[8] Science has provided a host of benefits including vaccines to protect us from polio, smallpox, measles, and other diseases. Science has developed antibiotics to help us fight off bacterial infections, medications to alleviate a host of diseases, and to extend life. Gene therapy using CRISPR, a gene editing technique, is like molecular surgery in which short DNA sequences can be cut out and replaced with ones that repair defects. A CRISPR technique has just been approved by the FDA for curing sickle cell disease.

The Reverand Billy Graham's thoughts on Scripture and Science

> *"I don't think that there's any conflict at all between science today and the Scriptures. I think that we have misinterpreted the Scriptures many times and we've tried to make the Scriptures say things they weren't meant to say. I think that we have made a mistake by thinking the Bible is a scientific book. The Bible is not a book of science. The Bible is a book of Redemption, and of course, I accept the Creation story. I believe that God did create the universe. I believe that God created man, and whether it came by an evolutionary process and at a certain point He took this person or being and made him a living soul or not, does not change the fact that God did create man. [...] whichever way God did it makes no difference as to what man is and man's relationship to God."* (Billy Graham (1918–2018), evangelist, pastor, and author.[9] This quote which agrees with the views expressed above was found late in the writing of this book.

Good News in the Gospels

The Gospel is the Good News that Jesus Christ the Son of God came into the world and taught us to love one another then He

---

8. Hall, "Building Phylogenetic Trees," 1229–35.
9. Frost, *Billy Graham*, 72.

died for the forgiveness of our sins. The Good News is found in the Gospels of Matthew, Mark, Luke, and John, not in Genesis. Bibles could be better arranged by putting the New Testament first, followed by the Old Testament. Bible translation organizations, such as Wycliffe and Pioneer, focus on first translating Mark into languages that have never had a Bible in their native language. The Gospel of Mark is the shortest and presents the core message of the Christian faith. Some Christians are overly focused on prophecy scriptures, such as those in Daniel and Revelation. Creation scientists are not working to understand diseases to help the sick, nor are they feeding the hungry. They are making money based on fake "discoveries" that they sell as creation science to those who believe that God created the World, but they do not understand scientific methods and often believe what they are told rather than carefully reading scripture.

God the Creator was a brilliant chemist and molecular biologist to have made this wonderful world, using just four nucleotide bases of DNA and only twenty amino acids. *"It is the faithfulness of God that allows epistemology to model ontology."* - John Polkinghorne, professor of mathematical physics at the University of Cambridge, theologian, and Anglican priest.[10] This quote simply states that since God is dependable and consistent (faithful), the way we learn about the world through science (epistemology) can accurately reveal truths concerning our world and the cosmos (ontology). The sciences, such as mathematics, chemistry, physics and biology, provide rules and methods for learning about our physical world. God keeps things simple! He gave Moses just ten commandments that man struggles to keep. Then Jewish leaders added hundreds more laws that made life extremely complicated. Jesus the Great Physician fulfilled the law and then He simplified it by giving only two commands, *"Jesus replied: "'Love the Lord your God with all your heart and with all your soul and with all your mind.' This is the first and greatest commandment. And the second is like it: 'Love your neighbor as yourself.' All the Law and the Prophets hang on these two commandments."* (Matthew 22: 37-40, NIV).

10. Polkinghorne, "Faithfulness of God".

The New Testament is the "Good News," and Christians should focus on its messages. Missionaries share the Good News of the New Testament gospels, whereas creation scientists emphasize Genesis. Requiring belief in Old Testament stories is akin to the early Jewish Christians who were insisting that new believers be circumcised and follow Jewish law. Some Jewish Christians were arguing for circumcision and following other Jewish laws, which resulted in considerable debate among the early church members. Peter settled the debate as recorded in Acts. *"The apostles and elders met to consider this question. After much discussion, Peter got up and addressed them: "Brothers, you know that some time ago God made a choice among you that the Gentiles might hear from my lips the message of the gospel and believe. God, who knows the heart, showed that he accepted them by giving the Holy Spirit to them, just as he did to us. He did not discriminate between us and them, for he purified their hearts by faith. Now then, why do you try to test God by putting on the necks of Gentiles a yoke that neither we nor our ancestors have been able to bear? No! We believe it is through the grace of our Lord Jesus that we are saved, just as they are."* (Acts 15:6–11, NIV) Peter's rejection of circumcision and Jewish law as requirements for salvation allowed Christianity to spread around the world.

CHAPTER 18

Interesting Scientific Facts

"Science is built upon facts, as a house is built upon stones. But the facts themselves are nothing, without the cement of theory to bind them together."

—THOMAS HUXLEY, BIOLOGIST[1]

Viruses are Not Alive

VIRUSES ARE NOT CONSIDERED life forms because they cannot grow or replicate by themselves. They must use the machinery of the cells they infect to replicate or multiply. Viruses can use either DNA or RNA as their genetic material and when viruses infect, they steal the metabolic energy of the infected cells and take control of cellular machinery to replicate their genetic material and make their viral coat proteins. Approximately 70% of human viruses use RNA as their genetic material, with the rest using DNA. RNA viruses cause the common cold, influenza, COVID-19, HIV, hepatitis C, Ebola, rabies, polio, mumps, and measles. Well-known double-stranded DNA viruses that infect humans include chickenpox, shingles, smallpox, and hepatitis B. Some viruses, such as

---

1. Huxley,"Collected Essays".

parvovirus, have single-stranded DNA, and a few DNA viruses cause cancer.

Mad Cow Disease and Alzheimer's

One might think that Mad Cow Disease and Alzheimer's are an odd couple, but both are neurodegenerative disorders that affect the brain. Both involve the accumulation of misfolded proteins in the brain, but they differ regarding brain pathology, transmission, and causes.

Mad Cow disease is more properly termed Bovine Spongiform Encephalopathy (BSE). Dr. Stanley Prusiner discovered prions, a class of infectious self-reproducing pathogen proteins that he named prions based on the words "proteinaceous" and "infectious." It was exceedingly difficult to prove that proteins were infectious agents, rather than some viral contaminants and many scientists were very skeptical of Prusiner's research. New ideas are always slow to catch on, but he eventually presented adequate evidence and he won a Nobel Prize in 1997 for discovering prions. Prion proteins are misfolded and cause disease when they enter the brain and cause normal proteins to copy their misfolding and form polymers. Prions have more beta-sheet structure than do their normal alpha helical-rich counterparts and the normal protein alpha helix changes to beta-sheet upon binding to the disease prion. The beta sheet-rich prions tend to aggregate and polymerize, and those aggregates are visible in microscopic sections of infected brains. Sheep have long been known to have scrapie, a neurological condition that causes them to scrape themselves against fences, etc. There was an epidemic of BSE in England from 1987 – 1997 resulting in 180,000 cows with BSE. Evidence suggests that they became infected with prions after eating feed that contained neurological tissue from sheep with scrapie as a way of adding protein to the feed. Only 175 people from 1996–2011 contracted a rare and fatal neurological disease called variant Creutzfeldt-Jakob disease (vCJD). Once the BSE cattle were destroyed and the cause of BSE was recognized and corrected, the epidemic of vCJD slowly disappeared. Blood banks in the US would not take blood from individuals who had spent three months or more in England from 1980 through 1996, this precaution resulted in my not being able to donate blood after the vCJD epidemic. Fortunately, that precaution no longer exists.

Kuru is a prion disease of the Fore ethnic group of Papua New Guinea thought to have been propagated via ritualistic cannibalism of infected people. The disease can take up to 50 years to develop, resulting in tremors, jerky movements, dementia, and behavioral changes. Fortunately, it was eliminated when the practice of cannibalism ended. How prions enter the vasculature and travel to the brain remains a mystery.

Alzheimer's disease involves the accumulation of beta-amyloid plaques in the brain that are derived from amyloid precursor protein (APP), a transmembrane protein thought to be involved in neuron growth and survival. Amyloid plaques are thought to be similar to prions because they are beta sheet-rich aggregates in the brains of patients who died of Alzheimer's. Therefore, drug development has focused on preventing or removing beta amyloids from the brain. Alzheimer's is not thought to be transmissible and only affects humans. Amyloid plaques in Alzheimer's are made of aggregated misfolded amyloid beta (Aβ) proteins that disrupt normal neurological functions. While they are somewhat like prions, they appear unable to multiply in the same way that prions do.

Several other diseases involve protein aggregates. For example, the pancreatic beta cells secrete amylin along with insulin, and amylin clumps are found in the pancreas of Type 2 diabetic patients. Huntington's disease involves the aggregation of beta sheet-rich mutant Huntington protein resulting in neuronal damage. Emphysema can result from the inheritance of two mutated A1AT genes because A1AT normally protects the elastin-rich lung alveoli from damage by neutrophil elastase. A1AT is made by the liver and secreted into the blood where it travels throughout the body, but the mutant protein tends to form aggregates in the liver, resulting in abnormally low amounts of A1AT in the blood, leaving elastase free to damage the lungs.

CHAPTER 19

Science Gives Hope

"It is therefore clear to all unprejudiced minds that medicine is turning toward its permanent scientific path. By the very nature of its evolutionary advance, it is little by little abandoning the region of systems, to assume a more and more analytic form, and thus gradually to join in the method of investigation common to the experimental sciences."
—CLAUDE BERNARD, FRENCH PHYSIOLOGIST[1].

"Nothing in life is to be feared, it is only to be understood. Now is the time to understand more, so that we may fear less."
—MARIE CURIE[2]

Science and Hope

JUST AS THE RESURRECTION of Jesus Christ gave humanity hope for the future, scientists and engineers spend every day hoping for a breakthrough that will improve our understanding of how things work, including our bodies, our minds, our environment, and our

---

1. Bernard, *"Introduction À L'étude"* 25.
2. Curie, "Nothing in life."

Science Gives Hope

universe. Understanding science and the teachings of Jesus Christ leads to ways of improving life for everyone. When my parents were born around 1915 their life expectancies were about 53 years, for my generation born around 1945 it was 63 years, and those born today are expected to live on average 79 years. Many of these gains are due to improved sanitation, antibiotics, antivirals, and more knowledgeable physicians. New drugs, treatments, therapies, and surgical techniques are constantly being developed. Penicillin, the first antibiotic, saved my life when I was 5 years old. In 1915 most people were farmers and rural America had no electricity, no running water, and no indoor toilets. My grandfather plowed his fields with a mule. Additionally, advances in medicine and healthcare have not only extended life, but they have also improved our quality of life. The USA leads the world in scientific innovation. The biotechnology industry which is catalyzed by National Institutes of Health research grants provides 7 million jobs and adds $69 billion to the US GDP each year. NIH awards some 60,000 grants yearly that support over 300,000 researchers at 2,500 institutions. Discoveries are improving health and fighting disease. Human genomics supports over 850,000 jobs, and contributes over $265 billion in total economic impact yearly, with a return on investment of $4.75 for each $1 spent.[3]

Vaccines Prevent Disease and Save Money

Vaccinations have eradicated smallpox and almost conquered polio. When I was eight years old the polio epidemic was at its zenith with 57,000 cases and some 35,00 children paralyzed and many were confined to "iron lungs" to keep them alive. Iron lungs were large cylinders from which only the head was out. An air-tight rubber collar allowed the changes in positive to negative pressures inside the cylinder to move the diaphragm for inhaling and exhaling. The Salk vaccine was an injectable inactivated (damaged) poliovirus that became available in 1955. This was followed in

---

3. Health, "Impact of NIH Research."

1960 by the Sabin vaccine which was a live-attenuated virus vaccine (weakened live poliovirus) that was oral and often given on a sugar cube. Effective vaccines are now available for Chickenpox (Varicella), Hepatitis A and B, Human papillomavirus (HPV), Influenza (trivalent against three strains), MMR (Measles, Mumps, and Rubella or German measles), Pertussis (Whooping cough), Rabies, Rotavirus, Shingles, Tetanus, Yellow fever, Diphtheria, Hemophilus influenza type b (Hib, causes meningitis), Meningococcal meningitis, Pneumococcal disease (against 23 types of pneumonia), Typhoid fever, and COVID-19. These and others are constantly being improved.

Vaccines reduce disease severity, as well as prevent diseases. One might still "get the flu" or "get COVID" but you are more likely to survive if you are vaccinated. During the 2019–2020 flu season, the CDC estimates that influenza vaccination prevented 7.1 million illnesses, 3.45 million medical visits, 100,000 hospitalizations, and 7,200 deaths, considerable savings in suffering, medical costs, and lost productivity. The combined benefits of less illness, fewer hospitalizations, fewer deaths, increased productivity, and longer lifespans, are significant, yet immeasurable.

RNA Vaccines, asRNA, and siRNA Drugs

Knowledge and understanding of RNA led to the development of the first COVID-19 vaccines. RNA vaccines are being developed to prevent or treat malaria, melanoma, glioblastoma, Zika virus, HIV/AIDS, and other viruses and cancers. Antisense RNA (asRNA) that binds to its complementary mRNA to form a double-stranded RNA molecule is just beginning to be used. The double-stranded RNA is degraded, and/or it prevents the mRNA from being used to make the protein it codes for. The FDA has approved an asRNA therapy called nusinersen (SPINRAZA® marketed by Biogen) to treat spinal muscular atrophy. Other asRNA molecules are being developed to treat cancers, Alzheimer's, Huntington's disease, heart disease, HIV/AIDS, and Duchenne muscular dystrophy.

New small interfering RNA (siRNA) molecules are beginning to be used as drugs. Currently, four FDA-approved siRNA drugs trigger the degradation of target mRNAs, leading to significantly lower levels of the proteins that would normally be synthesized on ribosomes. For example, Leqvio® made by Novartis Pharmaceuticals prevents the synthesis of a protein that normally degrades low-density lipoprotein (LDL) receptors, responsible for clearing "bad cholesterol" from the blood. Since the LDL receptors are not degraded, they continuously remove LDL cholesterol from the blood. HDL cholesterol is called "good cholesterol", those with higher levels of HDL have fewer heart attacks. The siRNA has a special chemical modification that makes it highly stable and allows it to bind to specific proteins in the liver, so it only needs to be given by injection twice yearly.

Monoclonal Antibodies

Our understanding of the immune system and the development of monoclonal antibodies have produced new drugs. Monoclonal antibodies, such as Adalimumab (Humira), are revolutionizing medicine because they bind their targets with great specificity.[4] Monoclonal antibodies are proteins and are given via injection because the digestive tract cleaves them into individual amino acids. Additionally, generic names for all monoclonal antibody drugs end in "mab". Humira is used to treat rheumatoid arthritis, ulcerative colitis, Crohn's disease, and several other autoimmune conditions by binding up the pro-inflammatory protein called tumor necrosis factor-alpha (TNF-alpha). The functional part of the Humira protein molecule was developed by immunizing mice, but the great majority of Humira is like many other antibodies that our immune system makes, and its humanness prevents rejection. AbbVie's sales of Humira have exceeded $200 billion since 2002, and generic (biosimilar) versions are now being sold.

---

4. Jamal, "Adalimumab Response," 413–9.

Synthetic Peptide Drugs

At present sales of new drugs to treat type 2 diabetes and obesity are booming. The body makes several peptide hormones that are cut from larger protein precursors by specific proteases. Insulin is one example that has been discussed. These new drugs are polypeptides about thirty amino acids long that mimic the functions of glucagon-like peptide-1 (GLP-1) and/or glucose-dependent insulinotropic polypeptide (GIP). They are produced via recombinant DNA technology in yeast or bacteria. Modifications of some amino acids prevent their degradation by peptidases (proteases). Additionally, they have lipophilic fatty acid chains attached for binding to blood serum albumin which increases their duration of function up to a week. They also suppress the desire for food and slow food movement through the digestive tract. Like insulin, they must be given by injection because they would be destroyed in the digestive tract. The success of these drugs has increased research to produce more polypeptide drugs.

CRISPR-Cas9

CRISPR-Cas9 is an innovative technology that allows scientists to "erase" a DNA base and replace it with a different base. Cas9 is like tiny scissors that clip out pieces of DNA and CRISPR directs to the "bad" DNA segment that is then replaced with the normal DNA sequence. This technology can replace a faulty gene sequence with the corrected version. The FDA has approved the CRISPR-Cas9 process that cures sickle cell disease which shortens lives, causes severe pain, and requires multiple hospitalizations. Since it has been long known that sickle cell patients who continue to make low levels of fetal hemoglobin are not as sick with this disease, CRISPR-Cas9 was used to modify hemoglobin genes in red blood cell precursors so more fetal hemoglobin was produced thus stopping the disease process.[5] This and other approaches are being worked on to cure a host of diseases due to genetic defects.

5. Sharma, et al. "Crispr-Cas9 Editing," 820–32.

Currently, work is progressing on gene therapies for beta-thalassemia (another hemoglobin gene mutation), hemophilia, cancers, cardiomyopathies, arrhythmias, cystic fibrosis, Huntington's disease, Alzheimer's, and blindness due to Leber congenital amaurosis and retinitis pigmentosa. Other potential uses are to improve agricultural products, plants, and animals.

As we have seen with the development of nuclear energy and social media, new technologies can be used for good or evil. Gene editing can be used to cure diseases but also to make designer babies or biological weapons. The United States has done an excellent job regulating and overseeing the uses of gene editing via the FDA, NIH, USDA, and EPA. Universities, biotech companies, and research institutes have Institutional Review Boards that must review projects for ethical use and the protection of human subjects. These boards include ethicists, non-scientists, and others charged with preventing scientific or social research from being misused. Personally, my biggest concern is the possibility of misuse in foreign countries that do not share our morals and Judeo-Christian ethics, particularly communist countries.

Artificial Intelligence (AI)

AI is in the news and will be for years to come. It is a little scary and powerful. ChatGPT, Gemini, Bing Copilot, and Perplexity are various AI chatbots that I have used or explored. While they can produce erroneous information, I have found them useful and like their detailed responses.

The gold standard for determining the 3D structure of a protein has always been X-ray diffraction of protein crystals, which involved considerable experimentation to obtain crystals, followed by the collection of X-ray diffraction data, and finally, analysis of the data to produce a protein structure based on atom location in 3D space. Biochemists and computer scientists have been working for years trying to accurately predict protein structures. In 1992 I spent two months in The Laboratory of Molecular Biophysics at Oxford University modeling the 3D structure of human mast cell tryptase. First, we performed a multiple sequence alignment of the tryptase amino acid sequence with that of bovine trypsin. We then performed homology modeling of tryptase based on the structure of trypsin, being careful to position the active site amino acids (His, Asp, and Ser), exactly as they are positioned in trypsin. Our biggest problem was modeling a short sequence in tryptase that did not align with any of the sequences in trypsin. This work required Silicon Graphics computers which were the only ones with the capability of displaying detailed protein structures. Since then, sales of PCs capable of gaming have reduced the prices of machines capable of displaying complicated molecular structures. Our model was far from perfect, but in 1992 we published the model in Protein Science[6] the journal of the Protein Society.

AI has resulted in a great leap forward in predicting protein structures. AlphaFold developed by DeepMind, a subsidiary of Alphabet, directly predicts the 3D structures of proteins with considerable accuracy. AlphaFold2[7] uses a deep learning technique that focuses on having the AI piece together protein structures based on the known structures of thousands of proteins. This and similar AI-powered processes will improve understanding of protein-protein interactions and of drug interactions, which should lead to the development of new drugs and the repurposing of existing drugs and other chemicals. As with all new technologies, there is the potential for misuse. The atomic bomb ended World War II by destroying two Japanese cities and killing thousands of people, yet it is estimated to have saved many American lives and shortened the war by months. In schools, we had practice drills in case of nuclear attacks huddling under our desks, which would have not protected us at all. Nuclear power plants have provided electricity for years with only a few accidents. Over thirty firefighters died at Chernobyl from radiation sickness, and there have been other nuclear accidents. Radiation treatments for cancers are now commonplace and new nuclear power plant designs should reduce accidents. AI should be useful in controlling nuclear power plants to

6. Johnson and Barton, "Mast Cell Tryptases," 370–7.
7. Baek et al. "Accurate Prediction of Protein." 871–76.

make them safer. Fortunately, nuclear bombs have not been used in war or terror attacks, even though the number of countries with nuclear weapons has increased. Like all innovative technologies AI can be used for good or evil, and I pray that we learn to control AI, as well as the harmful aspects of social media. "It is better to travel in hope than to arrive." This saying is based on Robert Lewis Stevenson's Roads Essay (1874) which states *"To travel hopefully is a better thing than to arrive, and the true success is to labor."*[8] By labor, he was referring to everyday life, our occupations, every breath, and time with friends and family. So, I enjoyed every step in drafting this book, and I continue to live each day in hope. *"May the God of hope fill you with all joy and peace as you trust in him, so that you may overflow with hope by the power of the Holy Spirit."* (Romans 15:13, NIV).

---

8. Stevenson, "Roads".

CHAPTER 20

A Personal Journey with Science and Faith

"To love means loving the unlovable. To forgive means pardoning the unpardonable. Faith means believing in the unbelievable. Hope means hoping when everything seems hopeless."
—G.K. CHESTERTON [1]

Education, Family, and Faith

MEMPHIS CITY SCHOOLS PROVIDED a solid educational experience, then I earned my B.S. and Ph.D. degrees in chemistry from the University of Memphis. My dad was a mechanic and machinist with the Memphis Fire Department and my mom was a secretary, and neither had attended college. When I was 11 years old, I accepted Jesus Christ as my LORD and Savior, and I was baptized by our minister Dr. A.D. Foreman. Memphis had such a good chemistry department that the American Chemical Society certified my B.S. degree. Being curious about how things worked led me to chemistry in college and biochemistry (life's molecules) in graduate school. Two summers after my B.S., I worked in the antigen preparation lab of the Centers for Disease Control (CDC)

1. Chesterton, "To love means."

in Chamblee, GA, and thus began my interest in lung disease. My Ph.D. dissertation research was on the "Purification and Properties of a Proteolytic Enzyme from *Escherichia coli*", and led to my interest in proteases. Then I moved to the University of Georgia in Athens to work with Dr. James Travis on human proteases and protease inhibitors involved with human lung disease. Awards of an NIH post-doctoral fellowship and then my own NIH grant allowed me to advance to Research Assistant Professor. During this period, I developed expertise in protein purification, affinity chromatography, amino acid analysis, and protein sequencing. My career in biochemistry during the last 50 years has been exciting and intellectually rewarding. Human proteins have been my primary interest because more knowledge about them contributes to improving health via a better understanding of their structure and function. My Curriculum Vitae lists sixty-seven publications, of which 65 were published in peer-reviewed scientific journals that can be found via PubMed. As Professor Emeritus of the East Tennessee State University Quillen College of Medicine my CV can be reached via the Department of Biomedical Education website.

Lung Biochemistry and Emphysema Research

Emphysema results from damage to the elastin-rich air sacs of the lung called alveoli. These tiny balloons expand each time we inhale and contract when we exhale. Alveoli are surrounded by a mesh of capillary blood vessels that absorb oxygen and release carbon dioxide (as a waste product of metabolism). Cigarette smoking is the primary cause of emphysema because inhaled smoke particles trick the body into defending the lungs as if these were invading organisms. Smoke induces neutrophils, which are our first line of defense against invading bacteria or yeasts, to move to the lungs to fight the smoke particles. Neutrophils swallow up bacteria and kill them by generating oxidants such as hydrogen peroxide and hypochlorite (bleach). They also use their proteases called Cathepsin G and elastase to digest microbial proteins. Additionally, pulmonary macrophages enter the lungs to help kill microbes and initiate an immune response, and they also have an elastase enzyme that they release. Neutrophils only live for about 24 hours. When they die, they release their content of oxidants and proteases, which can damage the lung structural proteins, particularly elastin, which enables the air sacs to expand and contract. In the early 1960s, a Swedish biochemist and a physician found that some young patients who were developing emphysema had low levels of a protein called A1AT. Further research in which elastase was placed in the lungs of animals showed that too much of this enzyme could cause emphysema and other experiments showed that the function of A1AT was to inhibit neutrophil elastase. A1AT is produced by the liver, but a mutation in its amino acid sequence causes it to aggregate (collect) in the liver, preventing secretion into the blood. People from northern Europe can have a genetic mutation in A1AT that reduces the secretion of A1AT from the liver and those with two copies of the mutant gene tend to develop pulmonary emphysema at an early age, especially if they smoke. My work with Dr. Travis at the University of Georgia focused on determining how A1AT inhibited elastase. After discovering that A1AT formed a tight bond with its target proteases, I started determining the amino acid sequence of A1AT. In 1977 I discovered the amino acid sequence of Alpha-1 Antitrypsin (A1AT) where neutrophil elastase binds in the inhibitory reaction.[2] This discovery was followed by experiments showing that oxidation of the methionine in the inhibitory site of A1AT reduced elastase inhibition. We hypothesized that oxidants in the lungs (inhaled and produced by neutrophils) could decrease the ability of A1AT to protect the lung from damage by elastase.[3] A1AT was the first of over thirty similar human proteins collectively called SERPINs (SERine Proteinase INhibitors), and over 1,500 similar proteins are now known to exist in various organisms. Interestingly, the protein that makes up most of the egg white that provides a source of amino acids for the growing chick embryo is a SERPIN, but it is not a protease inhibitor. It is my firm belief that God aided my research discoveries

2. Johnson, and Travis. "Structural Evidence for Methionine."
3. Johnson and Travis, "Oxidative Inactivation," 4022–6.

on A1AT. This hypothesis was later supported by the research of other scientists and remains the leading hypothesis concerning the pathology of emphysema caused by smoking or air pollution. It explains why smokers develop emphysema.

Research at East Tennessee State University

At East Tennessee State University my research was initially supported by the Council for Tobacco Research. Then the Health Effects Institute and the Environmental Protection Agency funded us to study the effects of the air pollutants (ozone and nitrogen dioxide) produced by automobiles on A1AT. The NIH and American Heart Association supported my work on human mast cell proteases and neutrophil proteases, resulting in the expression of active recombinant enzymes using the yeast *Pichia pastoris* as the host organism. Work in conjunction with Promega, a biotech company, resulted in human mast cell tryptase as one of their products. Human enteropeptidase (also called enterokinase) was also produced as a recombinant protein. The expression of recombinant human neutrophil elastase and human neutrophil cathepsin G eliminated the need to purify them from human tissues or blood, which are hazardous sources that may contain infectious agents, such as viruses.

With funding from the Wellcome Trust, a British charitable foundation founded in 1936, I spent three months in Cambridge in 1985 researching proteases and their inhibitors at Strangeway's Laboratory on Wort's Causeway. Wellcome also funded a short two-month research sabbatical in the Laboratory of Molecular Biophysics in Oxford to develop a molecular model of human mast cell tryptase. The American taxpayers generously provided financial support for my research programs on human proteins, and I thank you. It has been a privilege to help start a medical school in the southern Appalachian Mountains. This underserved region needed rural physicians and the effort was challenging, exciting, and rewarding.

Our Church, Faith, and Community

In 1979 my wife and I joined Boones Creek Christian Church (BCCC), founded in 1825. We were active members, serving in various capacities from teaching Sunday School to serving in leadership positions. BCCC has always emphasized God's love for all His creations and the importance of grace. Numerous friendships with other members continue to enrich our lives. When I was 70 years old, I was awakened in the middle of the night a few weeks before taking on the duties of serving as an elder at BCCC. The Holy Spirit was telling me to be baptized again. David Clark baptized me at the beginning of a BCCC Sunday morning service and I made the good confession of St. Peter, repeating after Pastor David, "I believe that Jesus is the Christ the Son of the Living God", I then added the words given to me in the middle of the night; "I also believe in baptism for the forgiveness of sin and for receiving the Holy Spirit." I think he was a bit surprised by that because most people just repeat the Good Confession after the minister.

One important thing I have learned is that I cannot fix other people because I cannot even fix myself. We tend to want justice for others, but mercy for ourselves. As a child I memorized John 3:16 (NIV) in Sunday School. *"For God so loved the world that he gave his one and only Son, that whoever believes in him shall not perish but have eternal life."* But I now think that John 3:17 (NIV) is just, if not more, more important. *"For God did not send his Son into the world to condemn the world, but to save the world through him."* Jesus did not come to condemn or judge us or anyone but to teach all to love and to see each person as a beautiful soul created by God. This message is seen throughout gospel stories in Jesus' actions and words. Yes, we humans are flawed in many ways, and we do things intentionally and unintentionally that hurt others, but we are forgiven by the grace of God, through the life, death, and resurrection of Jesus Christ.

While teaching during the COVID-19 pandemic, I discovered that students appreciated encouraging quotes. Here are some of my favorite quotes.

A Personal Journey with Science and Faith

"Judging others makes us blind, whereas love is illuminating. By judging others, we blind ourselves to our evil and to the grace which others are just as entitled to as we are."
—Dietrich Bonhoeffer.[4]

"Not all of us can do great things. But we can do small things with great love." —Mother Teresa.[5]

"Love one another." —Jesus (John 13:34, NIV)

Figures, images, and video preparation

Images were created by the author using PowerPoint, except for some that are in the public domain, which are not copyrighted were taken from websites such as Wikipedia, or US government websites and often modified for emphasis. Scriptures taken from the Holy Bible, New International Version®, NIV®. Copyright © 1973, 1978, 1984, 2011 by Biblica, Inc.™ Used by permission of Zondervan. All rights reserved worldwide. www.zondervan.com The "NIV" and "New International Version" are trademarks registered in the United States Patent and Trademark Office by Biblica, Inc.® The molecular images were generated from structures in the Protein Data Bank (PDB) using the free version of Discovery Studio software from Bovia, a division of Dassault Systèmes. Videos were made by recording a computer screen using TechSmith's Camtasia Studio to generate mp4 video files that were then uploaded to YouTube as Unlisted videos. Many of the images were made or modified using MS PowerPoint, which normally Exports images at only 96dpi by default. To change this to 300dpi needed for printing required editing an MS PowerPoint Registry key for which instructions can be found by asking Gemini AI or by searching for a YouTube video. Stable QR codes were generated by qrcodemonkey https://www.qrcode-monkey.com.

4. Bonhoeffer, "The Cost of Discipleship." 205–6.
5. Teresa, "Not All of Us Can".

My YouTube Channel

The following videos and several more about biochemistry and faith are on my YouTube channel: search for David A. Johnson, Ph.D., or @DrJQuillen. The four listed here provide more detail for further learning. You might also like to read "The Language of God: A Scientist Presents Evidence for Belief", by Dr. Francis Collins published in 2006 with the view that God's language is DNA.[6]

Original YouTube video based on my 2016 church communion meditation, titled **"God is Visible in the Molecules of Life - DNA and Proteins"**. The popularity of this video has resulted in YouTube placing ads on it.

God is Visible in the Molecules of Life Video

This video provides a more detailed explanation of **Hemoglobin A1c** and the damage to all the proteins in our bodies caused by glycation in which glucose attaches to hemoglobin and many other protein amino groups. Glucose increases in the blood when it is not being properly taken up by our cells. Diabetes causes a lot of health problems. Type 2 diabetes accounts for about 90% of the cases. Hemoglobin A1c is a measure of our glucose levels over

---

6. Collins, *Language of God*.

time because red blood cells live for 100–120 days, so it provides a 3-month running average. High A1c values tell your doctor that the proteins in your blood vessels, kidneys, and eyes (to name a few) are being damaged.

Hemoglobin A1c

Blood Clotting with more detail about platelets, enzyme cascade, and diseases. **Blood Clotting Made Simple** a simple graphic for understanding blood clotting via the intrinsic and extrinsic pathways that involve several arginine-specific serine proteases. and the drugs used to slow clotting. Factors 8, 5, and 3 are proteins that aid three of the enzymes. Factor 8 deficiency is hemophilia A, and factor 9 deficiency is hemophilia B. Thrombin converts soluble fibrinogen to fibrin, which forms the clot. Drugs that slow clotting are discussed.

Blood Clotting Made Simple

Factor 5 Leiden or Factor V Leiden is a genetic point mutation that accounts for about 50% of deep vein thrombotic (DVT) events. Blood clotting prevents us from bleeding to death from cuts, but the process must stop once the bleeding is under control. A mutation in Factor 5 prevents its degradation by activated protein C, which normally stops the further production of thrombin and stops clotting.

Factor 5 Leiden

Bibliography

Alberts, Bruce, et al. *Molecular Biology of the Cell (4th Ed.)* Garland Science (2002) 335. https://archive.org/details/AlbertsMolecularBiologyOfThe Cell4thEd/page/n335/mode/2up

Annan, Kofi. "Knowledge Is Power. Information Is Liberating. Education Is the Premise of Progress, in Every Society, in Every Family." (1967) Address at the World Summit on Information Society. 23 June. https://press.un.org/en/1997/19970623.sgsm6268.html

Arnold, Frances. "Nature is solving all sorts of problems that we throw at her - how to degrade plastic bottles, how to degrade pesticides and herbicides and antibiotics. She creates new enzymes in response to that all the time, in real-time." (2024). https://www.brainyquote.com/lists/authors/top-10-frances-arnold-quotes.

Augustine, Saint. "God Loves each of us as if there was only one of us." Brainyquote (2024). https://www.brainyquote.com/quotes/saint_augustine_105351.

———. " It was pride that changed angels into devils; it is humility that makes men as angels." Brainyquote (2024).

Baek, Minkyung, et al. "Accurate Prediction of Protein Structures and Interactions Using a Three-Track Neural Network." *Science*, 373, 6557, (2021) 871–76. doi:10.1126/science.abj8754.

Bernard, Claude. "Introduction À L'étude De La Médecine Expérimentale." vol. No. 2. Baillière, English translation, Henry Schuman, Inc. 1927, Routledge 2017, (1865) 25.

Bonhoeffer, Dietrich. "The Cost of Discipleship." Revised Edition, Macmillan Co., Inc. (1937) 205–06.

Bovy, Jo and Rix, Hans-Walter. "A Direct Dynamical Measurement of the Milky Way's Disk Surface Density Profile, Disk Scale Length, and Dark Matter Profile at 4 Kpc <~ R <~ 9 Kpc." *The Astrophysical Journal*, 779 (2013) 30. doi:10.1088/0004-637X/779/2/115.

Cawein, Madison, et al. "Hereditary Diaphorase Deficiency and Methemoglobinemia." *Arch Intern Med*, 113 (1964) 578–85. doi:10.1001/archinte.1964.00280100086014.

Bibliography

CDC. "Estimated Flu Illnesses, Medical Visits, and Hospitalizations Prevented by Vaccination in the United States - 2019–2020 Flu Season." https://www.cdc.gov/flu/about/burden-prevented/2019-2020.htm?CDC_AA_refVal=https%3A%2F%2Fwww.cdc.gov%2Fflu%2Fabout%2Fburden-averted%2F2019-2020.htm.

———. "Measles - for Healthcare Providers." (2024). https://www.cdc.gov/measles/hcp/index.html,

Chesterton, Gilbert K. "To love means loving the unlovable. To forgive means pardoning the unpardonable. Faith means believing the unbelievable. Hope means hoping when everything seems hopeless." (2024). https://www.azquotes.com/author/2799-Gilbert_K_Chesterton/tag/love.

Clegg, Daniel O., et al. "Glucosamine, Chondroitin Sulfate, and the Two in Combination for Painful Knee Osteoarthritis." *N Engl J Med*, 354.8 (2006) 795–808. doi:10.1056/NEJMoa052771.

Collins, Frances *"The Language of God: A Scientist Presents Evidence for Belief."* (2006) Free.

Collins, Francis. "Genes Are Effectively One-Dimensional." Brainyquote." (2024) https://www.brainyquote.com/quotes/francis_collins_555153.

Curie, Marie. "Nothing in life is to be feared, it is only to be understood. Now is the time to understand more, so that we may fear less." (2024). BrainyQuote. https://www.brainyquote.com/quotes/marie_curie_389010.

Dylan, Bob. "Bob Dylan, on This Day." Interview by Edna Gundersen, Lincoln, Nebraska, (1990) 31 August. https://alldylan.com/bob-dylan-on-this-day-august-31/

Edison, Thomas A. "I Didn't Fail 1000 Times. The Light Bulb Was an Invention with 1000 Steps." (2024). https://www.azquotes.com/author/4358-Thomas_A_Edison

———. "The Body Is a Community Made up of Its Innumerable Cells or Inhabitants." BrainyQuote (2024) https://www.brainyquote.com/authors/thomas-a-edison-quotes.

Einstein, Albert, "The World as I See It." John Lane The Bodley Head, Digital Library of India (1935) 28. https://archive.org/details/dli.ernet.247185/page/27/mode/2up?q=religious

———. "Zur Elektrodynamik Bewegter Körper". Annalen der Physik. 322 (1905) 891–921. doi:doi:10.1002/andp.19053221004. https://en.wikipedia.org/wiki/Time_dilation.

Frost, David. "Billy Graham: Personal Thoughts of a Public Man." Chariot Victor (1997) 72.

Ghofrani, Hossein A., et al. "Sildenafil: From Angina to Erectile Dysfunction to Pulmonary Hypertension and Beyond." *Nat Rev Drug Discov*, 5.8 (2006) 689–702. doi:10.1038/nrd2030.

Glaeser, Georg and Paulus, Hannes F. "The Evolution of the Eye." (2015) Springer. https://doi.org/10.1007/978-3-319-17476-1.

BIBLIOGRAPHY

Goran, Michael I., et al. "High Fructose Corn Syrup and Diabetes Prevalence: A Global Perspective." Glob Public Health, 8.1 (2013) 55–64. doi:10.1080/17441692.2012.736257.

Hall, Barry G. "Building Phylogenetic Trees from Molecular Data with Mega." *Mol Biol Evol,* 30,5 (2013) 1229–35, doi:10.1093/molbev/msto12.

Health, National Institutes of. "Impact of NIH Research." (2024) https://www.nih.gov/about-nih/what-we-do/impact-nih-research.

Khullar, Dhruv. "Faith, Science, and Frances Collins." (2022) April 7 The New Yorker. https://www.newyorker.com/news/persons-of-interest/faith-science-and-francis-collins,.

Hippocrates. "Let food be thy medicine and medicine be thy food." BrainyQuote. https://www.brainyquote.com/quotes/hippocrates_481260.

Huxley, Thomas Henry. *"Collected Essays" (1893-1894).* 5, Science and the Christian Tradition, (2011) Cambridge University.

Jamal, Shahin, et al. "Adalimumab Response in Patients with Early Versus Established Rheumatoid Arthritis: De019 Randomized Controlled Trial Subanalysis." *Clin Rheumatol,* 28.4 (2009) 413–9. doi:10.1007/s10067-008-1064-0.

Johnson, David A., and Geoffrey J. Barton. "Mast Cell Tryptases: Examination of Unusual Characteristics by Multiple Sequence Alignment and Molecular Modeling." *Protein Science,* 1.3 (1992) 370–7. doi:10.1002/pro.5560010309.

Johnson, David and James Travis. "Structural Evidence for Methionine at the Reactive Site of Human Alpha-1-Proteinase Inhibitor." *Journal of Biological Chemistry* 253.20 (1978) 7142–4.

———. "The Oxidative Inactivation of Human Alpha-1-Proteinase Inhibitor. Further Evidence for Methionine at the Reactive Center." *Journal of Biological Chemistry* 254.10 (1979) 4022–6.

King, Martin Luther, Jr. "Science Investigates Religion Interprets. Science Gives Man Knowledge Which Is Power Religion Gives Man Wisdom Which Is Control." (2012). "A Gift of Love: Sermons from Strength to Love and Other Preachings", 23, Beacon. https://www.azquotes.com/quote/159026?ref=science-and-religion.

Labbé, Ivo, et al. "A Population of Red Candidate Massive Galaxies ~600 Myr after the Big Bang." *Nature,* 616.7956 (2023) 266–69. doi:10.1038/s41586-023-05786-2.

Lancet, The. "Retraction--Ileal-Lymphoid-Nodular Hyperplasia, Non-Specific Colitis, and Pervasive Developmental Disorder in Children." *Lancet,* 375.9713 (2010) 445. doi:10.1016/S0140-6736(10)60175-4.

Landsteiner, Karl. "Ueber Agglutinationserscheinungen Normalen Menschlichen Blutes." *Wiener klinische Wochenschrift,* 14 (1901) 1132–34.

Lewis, Clive S. *"The Problem of Pain."* The Macmillian Company, (1947) 67–68.

Lind, James. *"A Treatise on the Scurvy".* A. Millar in the Strand, 1757.

Morris, Henry. *"That You Might Believe."* (1946) Revised ed., Good News, (revised 1985).

BIBLIOGRAPHY

Pauling, L. et al. "The Structure of Proteins; Two Hydrogen-Bonded Helical Configurations of the Polypeptide Chain." Proc Natl Acad Sci U S A, 37.4 (1951) 205–11. doi:10.1073/pnas.37.4.205.

Pauling, Linus. "Science is the Search for Truth, That Is the Effort to Understand the World: It Involves the Rejection of Bias, of Dogma, of Revelation, but Not the Rejection of Morality." AZ Quotes (2024). https://www.azquotes.com/author/11421-Linus_Pauling.

Perutz, Max. "A Discovery Is Like Falling in Love and Reaching the Top of a Mountain after a Hard Climb " https://www.azquotes.com/quote/573826.

Polkinghorne, John. "It Is the Faithfulness of God That Allows Epistemology to Model Ontology". John Polkinghorne (1998) https://www.azquotes.com/quote/1005692%22%20title=%22John%20Polkinghorne%20quote%22

Seattle, Chief. "Chief Seattle's Speech." The Seattle Sunday Star December (1854). https://www.csun.edu/~vcpsy00h/seattle.htm#:~:text=All%20things%20are%20connected%20like,God%20is%20also%20your%20God.

Shakespeare, William. "Romeo and Juliet.", Act 3, Scene 1, (1597) Oxford: published for the Malone Society (2000) Oxford University.

Sharma, Akshay, et al. "Crispr-Cas9 Editing of The." *N Engl J Med*, 389.9 (2023) 820–32. doi:10.1056/NEJMoa2215643.

Sigala, Desiree M., et al. "The Dose-Response Effects of Consuming High Fructose Corn Syrup-Sweetened Beverages on Hepatic Lipid Content and Insulin Sensitivity in Young Adults." *Nutrients*, 14, 8 (2022) 1648.

Stevenson, Robert Lewis. *"Roads" In Selected Essays of Travel by Robert Lewis Stevenson*. Charles Scribner's Sons., 1911.

Stone, N. and A. Meister. "Function of Ascorbic Acid in the Conversion of Proline to Collagen Hydroxyproline." Nature, 194 (1962) 555–7, doi:10.1038/194555a0.

Szent-Györgyi, A. "Observations on the Function of Peroxidase Systems and the Chemistry of the Adrenal Cortex: Description of a New Carbohydrate Derivative." Biochem J, 22.6, (1928) 1387–409. doi:10.1042/bj0221387.

Szent-Gyorgyi, Albert. " Water is life's matter and matrix, mother and medium…." (2023) https://www.azquotes.com/quote/119886?ref=water-of-life.

Teilhard, Pierre. "Pierre Teilhard De Chardin. Brainyquote "We are not human beings having a spiritual experience" (2024). https://www.brainyquote.com/authors/pierre-teilhard-de-chardi-quotes.

Teresa, Mother. "Quote "Not All of Us Can Do Great Things. But We Can Do Small Things with Great Love." (2021) United Nations postage stamp.

Twain, Mark. "The Only Way to Keep Your Health Is to Eat What You Don't Want, Drink What You Don't Like, and Do What You'd Rather Not." https://www.brainyquote.com/quotes/mark_twain_391585.

Wakefield, Andrew J., et al. "Ileal-Lymphoid-Nodular Hyperplasia, Non-Specific Colitis, and Pervasive Developmental Disorder in Children." *Lancet*, 351.9103 (1998) 637–41. doi:10.1016/s0140-6736(97)11096-0

BIBLIOGRAPHY

Watson, James D., and Andrew Berry. *DNA: The Secret of Life.* (2003) Knopf.

Watson, James D., and Francis H. Crick. "Molecular Structure of Nucleic Acids; a Structure for Deoxyribose Nucleic Acid." *Nature*, 171, 4356 (1953) 737-8.

www.ingramcontent.com/pod-product-compliance
Lightning Source LLC
Chambersburg PA
CBHW071610170426
43196CB00034B/2287